AÏM FOR
LIFE
MASTERY™

A HANDBOOK TO CREATE PEAK PERFORMANCE

AiM for Life Mastery™

The title of this book and the definition of peak performance used throughout are trademarks of our services. They have been used jointly and separately by Raymond Perras and his company, Repars Consulting Inc., since 1997 in dispensing various training and coaching services to a multitude of clients in both Canada and the United States.

No part of this book may be reproduced without the expressed written consent of the author or its representatives.

AuthorHouse™
1663 Liberty Drive
Bloomington, IN 47403
www.authorhouse.com
Phone: 1-800-839-8640

First published by AuthorHouse 10/13/2011

ISBN: 978-1-4670-3324-4 (e)
ISBN: 978-1-4670-3325-1 (hc)
ISBN: 978-1-4670-3326-8 (sc)

Library of Congress Control Number: 2011916783

Printed in the United States of America

Any people depicted in stock imagery provided by Thinkstock are models, and such images are being used for illustrative purposes only. Certain stock imagery © Thinkstock.

This book is printed on acid-free paper.

authorHOUSE®

This book is dedicated to my parents. Although my dad, my mother and my step-mother passed away many years ago, I owe my drive and focus for excellence to their uncanny and continuous way of urging me to be the best I could be. Ironically, I have reached this momentous milestone and they are not here to celebrate the result of their undying love and support for me.

I owe an eternal debt of gratitude to my mother for instilling in me a sense of nurturing during her terminal battle with cancer. She taught me at age eleven to care for my younger brothers and sisters after she was gone. This likely was the flame that flickered until I finally became aware of my mission to help others aim for peak performance.

Acknowledgements

The idea for this book had been simmering for many years. It has now become a reality in large part because of my two daughters, France and Joëlle, and my son Serge. Their continuous reminder of how I guided and coached them to be the best they can be, and how I could help others, finally convinced me that I should act. It was difficult to disregard and doubt the urgings of my children. Their continuous recollection of things they had learned which helped them avoid life's pitfalls caused me to develop new thinking pathways. Today, I thank them for believing and applying my fatherly advice over their adult life.

I would like to thank Tom Wentz for his significant contribution in helping to craft the concept of effort-less effectiveness. Back in 1999, Tom shared his concepts and philosophy about moving from mass production to mass customization in a book entitled "Transformational Change: How to transform Mass Production Thinking to meet the challenge of Mass Customization". Over the years, Tom has become a friend, confidant, and parallel thinker. I always benefit from his dry humour and quick wit in recognizing the "burned out but still shining" state of many people who have yet to recognize that peak performance is not the result of old thinking, but the progressive realization that we have all it takes to succeed. We just need to think differently!

The journey has been long and tortuous. If it were not for a special man who loved football, I probably would never have gotten this far. Larry Ring was the Head Football Coach at the University of Ottawa back in 1992 when I approached him to test some of my beliefs and techniques. He was open minded and seeking ways to raise the bar for the program. Through the four plus years I worked with him in peak performance, he allowed me to prove the concepts both at the coaching level and the individual player level.

I take pride in having been a part of his efforts to lead the revival of the University of Ottawa football program to national recognition with consecutive appearances in bowl games from 1995 to 1997. Larry remains a close friend and partner in creating a better world for those we touch.

Another person who deserves thanks for helping me rise to the pro ranks is Marcel Bellefeuille. In 1998, he followed Larry as the Head Coach for the University of Ottawa GeeGees. Partnering with him, we implemented a number of team and individual performance concepts that culminated into a National Championship in 2000. We were the Canadian Universities National Football Champions. That served as a springboard for Marcel to make it to the Pros. The journey had just begun. Since then, I've had the privilege of successively working with Marcel in the Canadian Football League in Regina with the Saskatchewan Roughriders, in Montreal with the Alouettes, and in Hamilton with the Tiger-Cats. Again, I was provided the opportunity to coach coaches and individuals in the finer points of teamwork, team building, and leadership aimed at peak performance.

On the business side, I could name many people who provided an opportunity to share my expertise and knowledge both as a consultant and a coach, and helped me gain more clarity in applying the process. The person who stands above all, both as a client and a user of my process is Bruno Lindia. I owe him a world of gratitude for believing in me, understanding the peak performance concept, and more than anything, proactively integrating it into his company, DMA Canada, and in his personal belief system. Through his continued and focused application of peak performance principles, Bruno has involved a number of people in raising the bar for themselves and their organizations. Many of his clients were referred to me for life mastery coaching. I will be eternally grateful for that mark of trust and confidence which has strengthened my belief in the value of peak performance coaching.

In professional sports, I have had the privilege of working with numerous athletes and see their performance rise in a major way through the application of the peak performance process. One in particular is Corey Grant, retired Canadian Football League receiver. In February 2004, I was asked by his coach to work with him in order for him to regain his confidence. Corey was a true professional. He dutifully learned the concepts and applied them in a focused and sustained manner. After his confidence had been practically destroyed the year before in one disastrous play, Corey became a most reliable receiver and completed his career in stellar fashion. I owe him for providing references to people he knows like "...I know a very good coach if not the best in the field." when telling them about me as a peak performance coach. Corey is not only a consummate pro, but also a remarkable man who has designed his life in line with the peak performance process. His vision is guiding him to success in his current career.

Another man to whom I am grateful is Casey Printers, a pro football quarterback who transformed his life through peak performance coaching. Casey has totally integrated the concepts into his daily routine and aligned his life on a personal vision that makes him much more than a pro football player. I'm thankful for the privilege of walking with Casey through the trials and tribulations of his career as a life coach, and helping him find the path to his personal accomplishments. Over the years that I've worked with Casey, we've developed a bond that is priceless. His insights and the personal experiences he has shared have allowed me to create ways and means to further help a client in mastering the peak performance process both in business and in sports. I particularly appreciate his total honesty in telling me "I don't know coach" when faced with a challenge. That spurs me on to be creative and find new ways of helping him view his life obstacles differently. I will always be grateful to him for forcing me to dig deeper into the knowledge and details of peak performance to support him on his journey to excellence.

I wish to thank two people for providing their insight in editing the book. André Vermette, a college confrere, who is a senior communications advisor with the Government of Canada provided his expertise in formatting and formulating my ideas into readable content. The other is my life companion, Louise, who diligently cast her eagle eye on the grammar and punctuation to make the book as conversational as possible.

A word of thanks also goes to Wally Kozak, a friend, a mentor, and a model of coaching. I bless the day when I met Wally who has been coaching peak performance for ages it seems. He provided the confirmation that the concepts, techniques and ideas I had accumulated over time were indeed the key to doing **the right stuff, in the right amount, at the right time**[TM].

Finally, to the many people I've worked with, and those who have read the draft and provided comments, thank you so much for being in my life and helping me gain perspective on a subject I feel very strongly about. If people applied the concepts of peak performance for life mastery just once every day, ultimately, the world would be transformed. This has been proven over and over again by those I've coached who have created a better life for themselves, and for those around them.

I wish you insight and clarity of thought as you travel through this book and gain awareness of a method to integrate peak performance, **the right stuff, in the right amount, at the right time**[TM].

AÏM FOR LIFE MASTERY™

Table of Contents

AÏM FOR LIFE MASTERY™

AÏM FOR LIFE MASTERY™

AÏM FOR LIFE MASTERY™

A Roadmap to
Peak Performance

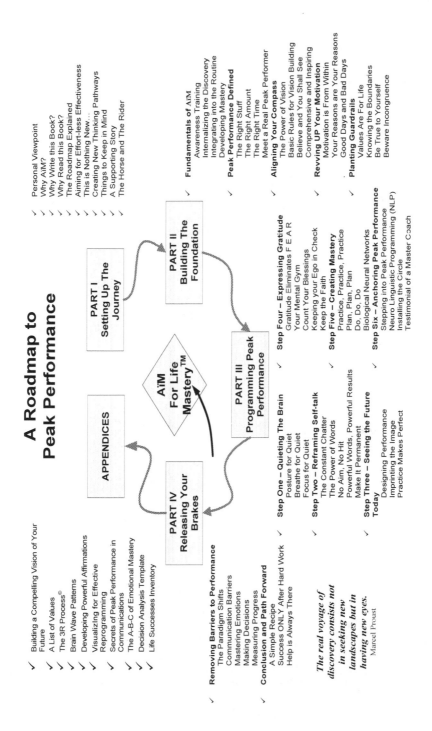

PART I
Setting Up The Journey

PART II
Building The Foundation

APPENDICES

AiM For Life Mastery™

PART III
Programming Peak Performance

PART IV
Releasing Your Brakes

The real voyage of discovery consists not in seeking new landscapes but in having new eyes.
Marcel Proust

AÏM FOR LIFE MASTERY™

Foreword

Once upon a time….. there was this boy from St-Charles, a little town in northern Ontario, Canada, 40 kilometers (25 miles) east of Sudbury. Born the third child of a family of eight, he enjoyed growing up on the farm, playing with his brothers and sisters, working in the gardens in summertime, shoveling snow in winter. Playing hockey as if he were Rocket Richard, he was imparted the love of sports by his mother who listened to the Montreal Canadiens on a battery-operated radio (we did not have electricity yet). Electricity came in 1950. I'm dating myself, but you get the picture. It's been a long road to the present.

Many years of experience, gathering knowledge, and becoming familiar with the finer realities of life have come and gone. How far has it been from the worry-free life of a child on the farm, enjoying nature, playing and learning to love animals, developing awareness of family, and experiencing the highs and lows of human interaction?

Well, it took many a disappointment and exhilaration, discoveries, learning the hard way, exceeding expectations, and also, I must admit, missing my goals. I was privileged to receive a sound education from my parents and the teachers who saw potential in me. They gave me some solid reference points to live my life by. With time, I woke up to the fact that we are indeed, masters of our destiny.

Some significant events marked my awakening along the way. None were more impacting than the death of my mother at eleven years old, and the marriage break-up I lived after sixteen years of happy married life and three beautiful children. Other events marked me, such as financial failure, and difficult attainment of business and career goals. Perhaps, the most enlightening event was my encounter with cancer at the age of 57. It provided the last push in getting me to share insight and help others gain life mastery.

AÏM FOR LIFE MASTERY™

Where It All Started

Way back in the 1980's, I competed in medium distance runs. In our preparation, I had the good fortune of meeting a sports psychologist who explained the principle of pain blocking to help us stay focused during a run. Running a long distance involves little aches and pains along the way. Developing the ability to block those sensations allows a person to continue at the same pace, and maintain endurance and a good form. As I learned, it is the power of our mind directing focus on the pain centre that creates an effect similar to a painkiller. The signal to the brain is affected, and the pain sensation subsides.

After I stopped competing, I got interested in finding out more about that mental principle. That's when I found out about accelerated healing, another mental process that frees our natural healing ability to heal our body. Throughout the years, I developed further understanding of how our brain works, and applied the techniques: relaxation to quiet the brain hyperactivity; affirmations to reprogram the subconscious thinking; visualization to anchor the new mental models; and a positive attitude through gratitude. I applied this knowledge to coach some athletes on how to deal with their injuries and come back on the field in half the usual time (accelerated healing is a mental process to remove obstacles that distract the brain from its main function: stress, desire to be on the field, lack of preparation for a return to action, etc.). As you read this book, you will get to understand the principles at work.

Over the years, after having coached athletes in a number of sports, I started to understand the saying that most top level athletes use when speaking of performance, "It's all mental." With time, I realized that I could help an athlete a lot more if I coached the mental preparation part of performance. Of course, that meant studying the field, and learning many techniques and processes to produce optimal results during performance.

AÏM FOR LIFE MASTERY™

My Cancer Story

Without going into a mountain of details, I wish to share part of my story at fighting cancer in the hope that you will feel the conviction I have about the power of our mind, and the reason why I've written this book.

Here is where that knowledge comes together in my fight with cancer. In the Spring of 2004, I discovered lumps in my neck, and they were not normal. I asked my doctor to check them out. He referred me to an ENT (ear, nose and throat) specialist who had a scan done. Something showed up, but could not be identified with confidence, so he called for a biopsy in early September. Throughout these checks, the doctor raised the possibility of cancer. Having seen both my parents die from cancer, I decided I was not going to let it happen to me. I started preparing mentally for the verdict. On September 26, 2004, the doctor confirmed the diagnosis – squamous cell carcinoma – back of the tongue, and the treatment was supposedly urgent. It was the morning of a day when I was travelling on business to Toronto by car.

Immediately after my momentous visit to the doctor, I took the road. As I had already prepared for the worst, I started right away to create new thinking pathways in my brain to kill the beast. Prior to receiving the results that day, I had chosen the words that would be my affirmation to guide my healing process. They were very fighting words: "Shutdown" and "Reject." I used the word "shutdown" to instruct my brain to stop the growth of cancer cells. The word "reject" was meant to drive my brain to command my body to get rid of the dead cells that would result from the shutdown process. I had also developed a video of the cancer killing action in my mind – a laser beam burning off the cells. I went to work on my subconscious brain to program it to fight on a continuous basis.

On November 1, 2004, I started radio and chemo therapies to treat the cancer as per the protocol the oncologist had designed. I followed that treatment till December 1st, every day, Monday to Friday. On that December day, I woke up and had to go to the hospital because my feeding tube (PEG) had become undone. When I got there, they immediately put me in isolation because I had a fever, and they established that I had contracted C-difficile; my immune system was giving up. I remained in isolation for thirteen days while they rescued me from infection. Needless to say, the cancer treatments were postponed for that period. At the time, I had roughly 60 percent of the prescribed treatment done.

While in isolation, you can imagine that I had a lot of time to think. Also, the lumps in my neck were gone. After many hours of analysis, I convinced myself that I could get rid of the cancer myself and prevent a total burnout. I was already losing the tips of my earlobes, and my neck was slowly turning a charcoal colour. So, on the tenth day of my isolation, when the oncologist came to visit, I told him that I was done with the treatments. Unless he felt that he needed to complete the radiation sessions to feel like he had done everything he could, I was going home and never coming back. He agreed with me after I explained how each treatment they had given me was amplified many times by the visualization I did every time I was under that machine. I told him how during each of the 20 minute treatments, I would visualize sparks flying as my brain directed the laser beam exactly where he had shown me the cancer was lodged.

The rest of the story goes like this. One month later, I started eating normally again, and two months after the premature end to the treatment, I was back to work full-time. During the ordeal, I had lost 35 pounds, so I was affected quite badly by the treatment, but my will to beat the cancer never weakened. A number of tests and follow up exams since January 2005, including X-ray scan, MRI and PET scan (positron emitting tomography) have failed to find any cancer cells in my body. To this day, I have the conviction that the process and techniques that I share with you in this book were the key ingredients of my victory over that deadly illness called cancer. And as a final note, I truly believe that cancer can never grow in me again. I have programmed my brain to reject anything that would resemble cancer growth.

The Driving Force

Strong from the personal experience of the power of the mind, I decided to pick up the gauntlet. I was determined to show that the lessons I had learned over a lifetime could be formulated to make them easier to

AÏM FOR LIFE MASTERY™

understand. What I will share with you is a process that ensures a productive life while requiring less effort. You will gain tremendous satisfaction in achieving your life goals with less stress. I've written this book to help you inject peak performance into your life!

Everything is a process. That's a concept I learned over the years as I observed people at work or at play. From getting up in the morning to go to work to getting ready for a presentation or preparing for performance in general, when you take a close look, the only way that results are produced is through a process.

I'd like to invite you on a journey through a process that will transform your life. So, sit back and let's share my secrets to becoming a peak performer.

AÏM FOR LIFE MASTERY™

PART I – SETTING UP THE JOURNEY

STAYING ON TRACK...

PART I   Setting Up The Journey

- ✓ Personal Viewpoint
- ✓ Why AÏM?
- ✓ Why Write this Book?
- ✓ Why Read this Book?
- ✓ The Roadmap Explained
- ✓ Aiming for Effort-less Effectiveness
- ✓ This is Nothing New...
- ✓ Creating New Thinking Pathways
- ✓ Things to Keep in Mind to Hike Your PERFORMANCE
- ✓ A Supporting Story
- ✓ The Horse and The Rider

PART II   Building The Foundation

PART III   Programming Peak Performance

PART IV   Releasing Your Brakes

APPENDICES

AÏM FOR LIFE MASTERY™

Introduction

It is not enough to do; sometimes, a person has to stop and realize that knowledge is meant to be shared. That's what happened to me. You may wonder why I'm making such a statement. Simple….. I continually see results beyond expectations happening to the people I coach. Consequently, I have come to the conclusion that more people can replicate those results. After all, aren't we all performers? No matter what your profession, art, trade, or life circumstance is, you're called upon to perform every day of your life. What if you had a simple recipe to help you increase your results while reducing stress? Let's explore how you can improve your performance by using some of your God-given talents more effectively.

Personal Viewpoint

Performance is largely linked to an automatic response.

*To better understand, let's think of breathing, blood circulation, digestion, healing, growing hair, all automatic responses to a central control system commonly known as the autonomous brain. It's a wonderful machine, always at work, driving our metabolic functions, our chemical equilibrium, fighting invaders through our immune system. And all that activity happens without one wilful conscious action from us. It's **"automatic"**.*

Isn't that wonderful? Ever stopped to think how all that happens inside you, and you don't do a thing to make it happen?

I've now passed my sixtieth birthday and have met many people from different walks of life. Even more importantly, I've witnessed in business and in sports numerous individuals who are otherwise high achievers in their career, but have created less than expected results because they were on what could be called "**automatic**". It's a reality of life that we often go through our daily routines without really being there. I mean present in mind, mindful of the context, the dynamics, the people, the human tendencies, the cultural differences, the ingrained beliefs, the results at stake. I had better stop.

Many factors are at play in most circumstances. If we are less than mindful in these circumstances, how many of these factors can escape our awareness and be overlooked in dealing with various situations? It's easy to understand how people can act on "**automatic**" most of the time. Now, don't get me wrong. Most people succeed very well "on automatic" because they have perfected their "**automatic**"!

However, I will submit to you that in some instances, depending on your personal experience, we don't reach the full potential of our efforts *BECAUSE* we are on **automatic**. After all, everything changes constantly. The last time we dealt with an issue will not necessarily repeat itself exactly. And so, we miss on those little extra results that can make a big time difference in the long run.

Why AïM?

> "In the long run, men hit only what they aim at. Therefore… they had better aim at something high."
> — **Henry David Thoreau,** author, poet, naturalist, and philosopher

I've chosen "**AïM for Life Mastery**™" as the title to illustrate the fact that few targets in life are hit without aiming. And aiming for life mastery is no exception. We can choose to be average, to be just like the next person, to have a normal life with its ups and downs, its successes and failures, and accept that, even if we could have done better, the result was "good enough". The fact is that life is pretty dull, and at times disillusioning if we learn to accept "good enough" without doing our best. The world is full of discontented people who have accepted "good enough" as their lot.

AÏM FOR LIFE MASTERY™

I submit that if you're seeking happiness, you must learn to have positive discontent, always seeking to be better than the last time out, giving it all you've got. Ask any top performer. They're happy when they've given their all, no matter the result. You see, it's not about the end of the road, but about how we travel on the road to the end result that creates happiness.

And thus, I've chosen to alert you to the fact that you must "aim" if you are to hit your desired results. This world is not perfect. Everyone encounters failure. But if you aim, you will hit more often, and that is the key to self-satisfaction = happiness.

The other part of the title alludes to the result of practice. With repetition, we usually get better and with time, we gain mastery. Isn't that the case for most everything we do? Mastery is more empowering than control. Control supposes constant effort to steer, to keep aligned, to avoid bumps in the road. It is compulsive, obsessive, and constraining. Quite the opposite, mastery is an automatic. Knowing how to do so well that it is freewheeling, smooth, propulsive, liberating, and totally by choice sure makes life more pleasant on the whole! Controlling ultimately makes us tired and weak, whereas mastering energizes us and gives us strength that we didn't realize we had. Witness the peak performers who accomplish unbelievable feats as if they were just ordinary events. Mastery does provide the edge that could be called "The Force".

So as you read the following chapters, think of the underlying meaning of the title – happiness through repeated and focused action.

You'll see on every page the reason why you're reading this book. Mastery is the **force** that can propel you to new levels of performance and so… may **The Force** be with you.

AÏM FOR LIFE MASTERY™

Why Write this Book?

Over the years, I've come to the conclusion that peak performance is not as easy as it might appear. What is EASY? Well, we may have the best intentions and wish to do our best, but often, unforeseen circumstances raise the potential for less than the expected results!

Let me explain.

In my coaching profession, I've had the privilege of working with a variety of people: students, professionals, ordinary folks, couples, athletes, sports coaches, business executives, technical experts, you name it.

> "Discovery consists of seeing what everybody has seen and thinking what nobody else has thought."
> — **Jonathan Swift**

It's amazing to discover how all these people are fully capable of dealing with their situation. They know their stuff and have the capability to create wonderful results. The most remarkable ability they possess is **awareness**. They have this uncanny ability to recognize the extent of their capabilities, abilities, skills and knowledge to face their challenges, and produce outstanding results at each and every turn.

However, as a budding coach, mentor, and parent, I've learned throughout the years to observe why people miss on their targeted performance.

More recently, in my role as a peak performance coach, I confirmed beyond doubt that the essence of performance lies within each individual. It is not the result of external factors. Oh yes, external factors have an influence, but only if a person lets the external factors affect him or her. My study is therefore

PP = the right stuff, in the right amount, at the right time™

AÏM FOR LIFE MASTERY™

directed at enabling you to develop the capability and capacity to deal with external factors in order to minimize their effect on your performance.

Over 30 years ago, I started reading about mental barriers and self-development. Every piece of information was stacked in my memory and tested in my everyday life – family, work, professional, social and community activities, even my finances! The more I became conscious of these barriers, the more my desire rose to help others develop their own peak performance approach.

Alas, it's one thing to have a "eureka" moment, and quite another to try helping someone else see the same perspective.

During my career as an engineer, I was fortunate enough to be able to use barrier awareness to inject perspective into the projects in which I was involved, and later as a manager, to guide my team along the same principles. My view was fortunately confirmed by the results I helped my teams achieve.

Here's an example of what I mean. In my first assignment as a leader responsible for an engineering team of ten people back in the early 1980's, I applied some of the notions about performance and coached my team to focus on their area of influence. We managed to produce 50 percent more work in the time that was given to us. I saw the results of people aligning their skills and abilities toward a common goal after barriers were removed – communication, teamwork, value-added work, effective use of resources, elimination of duplication, and most importantly, feedback to celebrate success and rectify deviations from the plan.

So, strengthened by actual confirmation of the teamwork I was fostering, I became convinced that I could show others how to apply a few key elements of self-direction to produce better results. Since 1990, I've looked for opportunities to share the fruits of my study and practical applications to help people increase their awareness and capability to create peak performance in their daily routine.

I've done this through life coaching in business and performance enhancement with athletes at all levels from minor sports to the pros, and with business people at various organizational levels all the way to the top.

My years of coaching people in a wide range of professions, age, status, domain of activity, and walks of life, has brought me to the realization that I have to share the same techniques with a wider audience. What better way than to write a short guide on proven techniques that will increase the results in your life!

Why Read This Book?

Now that I've piqued your curiosity, let me tell you how this book will provide a list of steps to create peak performance for your daily life. It will explain the exercises that are essential for you to develop new mental habits. As much as possible, you'll be provided with insight to help you understand the processes that might be at work, regardless of your circumstances.

I don't pretend to be a doctor or a psychologist, so I'll keep my explanations at a simple level. Where appropriate, I'll provide examples and references so that you may read up on the concepts or ideas I'm advancing. If you want to proceed as quickly as possible, this book will be your friend. The many cases I've encountered as a coach are distilled from the best understanding I have of the principles at work to create a new awareness. Many learned people have written about the subject and have articulated explanations and reasons why the "process" works. I'll refer you to a number of authors who have written extensively about their area of expertise. This book is not intended to recount their discoveries but is meant to point you in their direction where deemed necessary or appropriate.

AÏM FOR LIFE MASTERY™

The Roadmap Explained

You saw a roadmap to Peak Performance at the beginning of the book. This is aimed at making it easier for you to follow the process. The following briefly explains the segments of the path that you will follow if you want to reach peak performance in a systematic way.

However, you may choose to skip here and there throughout the book, and read about something that particularly catches your eye. Whichever way you decide to go, the roadmap will always be there to help you situate yourself in your journey toward peak performance.

Since I'm not there to answer your questions or guide your integration of the subject matter, the roadmap will help you keep all these concepts in perspective, and provide a sense of sequence in building the road to peak performance.

Roadmap for the Book Contents

Part I – SETTING UP THE JOURNEY

You've read about the origins of this book, and hopefully have gained insight regarding the perspective I've injected into the subject of peak performance. You probably have a fair idea of why I wrote the book - to share knowledge with those who seek to raise the bar, reach for better results while reducing their effort, and create a world of happiness for themselves and those around them.

I encourage you to return to the introductory words whenever you question yourself or my motive. Focusing on the mission (why?) will help you improve your understanding. After all, you're different from me, and your point of view is just as valid. However, in order to gain full insight into the method and process I'm putting forward in this book, it will be necessary to flex your mind a little, and seek to see things from the lens I am using to write about peak performance, and the journey which is involved in reaching that state.

There will be times when your beliefs will be stretched. What's in this book is not common knowledge even if it's part of your daily life. You will want to remember that any advance in our personal growth demands that we let go of certain ideas that we take for granted, unlearn past behaviours, and learn new ones that fit with our newfound awareness. My hope is that you will give yourself a chance to be touched by the new awareness this book can bring.

Part II – BUILDING THE FOUNDATION

Peak Performance is an ongoing journey that should become part of your daily life.

When I was younger, I didn't know yet that strength and accuracy come from sound knowledge of the task at hand. I remember the time when I first used a chainsaw. I had previously used a bucksaw to cut wood. I was so excited to finally be able to have a tool that reduced my effort. I soon found out the need to learn and understand how to use the machine before actually cutting the wood. Not knowing how to handle it, I got the saw pinched in a log and it kicked back, cutting the top of my left hand. Ten stitches and a hell of a scare were carved into my memory forever. I learned right then and there about the need to set the stage for peak performance!

The above example shows that, similarly, before you set off on a trek toward peak performance, you'll want to set the stage, prepare adequately, and equip yourself with a solid framework that will withstand the unexpected events in your life. The first five chapters are the details of the foundation you'll want to work on in order to ensure that your journey to peak performance is solidly anchored.

Understanding the **AÏM** concept, defining your direction, grasping the factors that motivate you, and ensuring that you have a means to stay focused on the road to success are essential ingredients in your recipe to become a peak performer!

All the ingredients upon which you will build a solid foundation for peak performance are described in this chapter.

Fundamentals of AÏM – an explanation of the acronym that represents the four parts of the approach to peak performance

Definition of Peak Performance – an explanation of the term as it is used in the book, and how it frames the guidance that the process provides you in your journey to peak performance.

Aligning Your Compass – any trip we take will be successful if we have clearly defined the desired endpoint. In the case of peak performance, like any endeavour, a clear and compelling picture of the future will decidedly keep you on the road to your goal.

Revving Up Your Motivation – not only do you need a clear view of the desired future but you also need to understand and integrate the reason why you want to reach that destination. Motivation is the fuel that will keep your engine going even in times of trials and tribulations (a.k.a. life's unexpected deviations from the goal).

AÏM FOR LIFE MASTERY™

Planting The Guardrails – like any road winding through treacherous terrain, your path to Peak Performance should be equipped with guardrails to help you stay on the road when slippery conditions (life's obstacles) show up. When the going is good, everything is fine, but when you encounter life difficulties, you'll need to have some strong reference points (values) to help you stay on course.

PART III – PROGRAMMING PEAK PERFORMANCE - THE MENTAL GYM

As with any project you undertake, once the foundation is built, you must put into action a series of actions that will strengthen your ability to deliver on your final product. In keeping with the concept that "practice makes perfect", the six chapters in this section explain the six steps of your mental practice to develop **Mastery** for Peak Performance. Consider these exercises to be very important in the achievement of your peak performance goal. Like riding a bike, playing golf, playing a musical instrument, or practicing your profession, to be your best, you must practice.

Here are the six steps to becoming a Peak Performer:

STEP ONE   **Quieting the Brain** – in order to set up for effective mental programming, the first step is to teach your brain to stop swirling around on command. Using the mind-body connection, you can learn to be calm and immobile in your body. You will automatically send a message to your brain to slowdown its activity. That's the state you want to create in order to have strong focus. One of the best methods is to control your breathing, a physical calming action that provides all kinds of benefits at the physical, emotional, and mental levels.

STEP TWO

Reframing Self-talk – once the brain is quieted, you can inject new thinking models through repetition of self-talk – guiding your inner voice to make it say what you want. It's a technique to sow good seeds in your subconscious brain, so that it produces good thoughts (positive) as opposed to weeds (negative thoughts) that usually cloud your thinking or even prevent you from thinking straight!

STEP THREE

Seeing the Future Today – it's not sufficient to talk to yourself. In every action that produces a successful result, you always have to see it in your mind before it actually happens. That's how our brain works. If you don't see it, you won't be able to get it done! Visualizing the result ahead of time allows you to create the mental and emotional states that will enable you to set your performance to the max.

STEP FOUR

Expressing Gratitude – you can program your subconscious to make yourself do whatever you want. However, you can greatly enhance this mental practice if you find a way to guide your subconscious brain away from the worry and fear of the future that is not aligned with what you want. It's a psychological principle that ensures proper focus in times of stress.

Develop the habit of being thankful for things in your life that bring you joy, satisfaction, or a feeling of gratefulness. Repetition works here too. With time, gratitude will push out all negative thoughts and allow you to eliminate the fear and worry that can paralyze you.

STEP FIVE **Creating Mastery** – this section summarizes the key to success in seeking peak performance. It brings all parts of the process into a whole. To gain mastery, there are no mysteries. You must PRACTICE. And to make the most effective and efficient use of your practice time, you should develop a routine – same time every day, twice a day. The key is to have short focused practices. Integrate the whole program into a heightened state of awareness where you live the desired state in your mind, body, and soul.

STEP SIX **Anchoring Peak Performance** – this section gives you a method that allows you to step into your performance state at will when it's required, including a testimonial that validates the concept.

PART IV – RELEASING YOUR BRAKES

The following sections summarize barriers that could present major obstacles to achieving peak performance.

Removing those barriers can go a long way to minimize efforts and maximize results. In a word, you can be more efficient in your journey to excellence. You can release your brakes and create new levels of achievement!

AÏM FOR LIFE MASTERY™

The Paradigm Shifts – an overview of seven paradigm shifts (changes in thinking) that will increase your effectiveness in your journey to peak performance. Changing your thinking can make the difference between a life of new discoveries and a constant perceived barrier to new horizons.

Communication Barriers – a number of barriers that reduce your communication effectiveness are reviewed to raise your awareness to the fact that applying some discipline and rigour can reduce the negative impact on your efforts to install peak performance!

Mastering Emotions – a simple recipe to corral the mental tendency to interpret events as being bigger than what they are, leading to a state of "overupset" which does not help peak performance! A simple thinking process is suggested to rectify what we tend to blow out of proportion, to "awfulize" as Jim Clemmer[1] would say.

Making Decisions – a short summary of some factors to consider when striving for peak performance. Lack of decisiveness in making choices is one 99of the biggest barriers to the attainment of peak performance.

Measuring Progress – a few words about the importance of creating feedback through reflection so that you generate motivation and momentum on your journey to peak performance. What gets measured gets done and repeated.

---

[1] Clemmer, Jim. *Growing the Distance.* TCG Press. 1999

AÏM FOR LIFE MASTERY™

CONCLUSION AND PATH FORWARD

A summary of the processes that create peak performance at will in your life. It's also a reminder of the key actions that will bring you to peak performance – constant and sustained effort to apply the peak performance principles in a uniform, consistent, and repeatable way. This is the most important thing to keep in mind when maintaining a firm direction toward peak performance in your life.

Once you learn to simplify the cause and effect relationship between focus and how you feel, you will master your own destiny! You will get closer to peak performance, with **the right stuff, in the right amount, at the right time**™.

APPENDICES

Additional reference material and tools

Now that you know how to navigate through the various parts of the book, let me go over a few additional concepts that will help you understand the perspective or lens through which the ideas are addressed. It will make your reading easier as these concepts provide added clarity to the text.

AÏM FOR LIFE MASTERY™

Aiming for Effort-less Effectiveness

I wrote this book with a clear intent to help you aim for **effort-less effectiveness** (peak performance). Over the years, I've observed countless people putting 110 percent (not really possible… just making a point!) in their effort to achieve. Unfortunately, the results were not always the best. And consequently, stress was part of their daily life. The deal is that more often

> **"Effort-less Effectiveness"**
> In this book, the word "effort-less effectiveness" is meant to describe the type of effort that leads to effectiveness with peak performance.
> It does not aim to say "no effort" but rather "less" effort when principles of peak performance are applied.
>
> Many thanks to my friend Bruno for clarifying the meaning of my thoughts!

than not, we work hard and produce less than expected results because we don't pay attention to the innate abilities we have, or don't use them in an effective, efficient and timely manner (**the right stuff, in the right amount, at the right time**™). So, I've set out to provide some insight that will help you increase the impact of your efforts while reducing stress. I want to share with you a method that will allow you to integrate **effort-less performance** in your daily life.

This is Nothing New

I want to alert you to the fact that nothing much is new here. It may seem new at the start, but you will find that the newness is only in the way that the concepts and ideas are organized and presented to help you design a path to peak performance. It's a structured and systematic approach to help you apply your existing knowledge, skills, and abilities to produce maximum results.

As you go through the book, remember Socrates' view on learning about our SELF. He said, "Learning is remembering what we already know."

Whatever you will read, remember that even if you don't think you have these abilities or understandings at the tip of your fingers, you are a person who is blessed with all the necessary life experiences to which the peak performance process refers to. It's just that you may not be fully aware of when and how they previously happened.

So don't be surprised to find yourself at times saying, "There's nothing new here". It will be a recall of your past experiences and life's lessons. My wish is that from now on, you will want to store those memories where you can recall them in a timely and effective fashion, and use them to the benefit of your end results. If you strive to do just that as you read the book, you will be way ahead of where you were when you started. You will facilitate a transformation in your thinking that will bring you closer to mastering Peak Performance.

As you read on, you will encounter facts and thoughts relating to the power of your subconscious mind. Pay attention. I'm sure you'll recognize their validity as you take time to reflect on your own experience. Be especially mindful of mental programming (or creating new brain pathways of thinking) which is one of the key premises of Peak Performance.

Creating New Thinking Pathways

Whether we like it or not, we are continually creating new thinking pathways (mental programs) for ourselves. We are also subject to being programmed and reprogrammed by events and people around us.

AÏM FOR LIFE MASTERY™

For example, just imagine if you did not know how to create new thinking pathways (programming) for yourself. How would you be able to learn to get up in the morning and prepare for the day? How would you be able to remember what you have to do next week? What you need to eat to be healthy? How would you be able to learn to ride a bicycle and not hurt yourself? How would you remember the route to go to your favourite hangout? The list is endless. That's the way our mind works.

Most of what we do has been carved in our brain (programmed) through repetition of an action to develop a mental model, a program that allows us to function effectively and deal with the daily events we encounter. And when we face something new, we use the pathways of our thinking process to evaluate, assess, and decide how to address the situation or issue.

We are continually creating new thinking pathways (programming and reprogramming) for ourselves. It is a wondrous capability of our brain to make sense of our surroundings and adapt through past experience. We are also creating thinking pathways (being programmed and reprogrammed) by repeated messages we receive from parents, educators, media and other communication processes including advertising.

Case in point. Back in the 50's, an infamous discovery of subliminal suggestion techniques exposed its use for commercials in movie houses. Visual commercials were filmed, then doctored to have split second pictures appear during the viewing. The human eye did not notice but the human brain picked up the attractive pictures, suggesting hunger, taste for, pleasure of eating, and drinking offerings. That way, movie houses ensured patrons visited the food kiosk and bought popcorn, chips, hot dogs and drinks, all without knowing it was being done to them. Do you think that the practice has stopped? It's likely that the methods have become more sophisticated, and we continue to get bombarded by subliminal advertising.

AÏM FOR LIFE MASTERY™

Marketing videos and other sales media continue to cause the creation of new thinking pathways (they program us).

What about two widely recognized brands that illustrate further how we are continually creating new thinking pathways? In the USA, people on the East coast say, "America runs on Dunkin' Donuts". It's an accepted fact that Dunkin' Donuts sells wonderfully succulent donuts and coffee that rivals Starbucks and Second Cup. In Canada, many people would not have a good day if they didn't get their "Timmy" from Tim Horton's in the morning. Every day, we see long lineups of people who have developed mental models that push them to drink that brand of coffee in an automatic way.

All this production of thinking pathways (programming and reprogramming) contributes to the evolving and ever-changing concept of our self-image.

Maxwell Maltz[2], an eminent American cosmetic surgeon, researched the impact of self-talk (programming) on self-image and self-esteem. Maltz believed that a person must have an accurate and positive view of his or her SELF before setting goals. Otherwise he or she will get stuck in a continuing pattern of limiting beliefs. He postulated that self-image is the cornerstone of all the changes that take place in a person. According to him, if one's self-image is unhealthy or faulty — all of his or her efforts to get ahead will end in failure. Obviously, it's important to watch our self-talk and how we continuously create thinking pathways in our brain.

Maltz's findings have been confirmed over and over in more recent works including the discoveries of Richard Bandler and John Grinder[3] on Neuro Linguistic Programming (NLP). Although the new science has its detractors, the fact is that the various

---

[2] Maxwell Maltz. *Psycho-Cybernetics: A New Way to Get More Living Out of Life.* Prentice Hall. 1960
[3] Bandler, Richard W. and Grinder, John T. *Frogs into Princes: Neuro Linguistic Programming.* Real People Press. 1989.

mental mechanisms at play can be quickly recognized once we pay attention to what is going on in our thinking process. Personal change is possible using self-programming.

If we accept the premise that new thinking pathways are being created all the time, doesn't it make sense to use this ability to guide your thinking process, and decide how you will react in certain given circumstances? Should you not attempt to reduce the number of times when you act, and then live to regret it, or wish you had behaved differently?

Why not make use of a natural ability to make your life a lot easier to live? Learn how to use self-talk to create thinking pathways that will enable you to effectively reach peak performance.

Things to Keep in Mind to Hike your PERFORMANCE

As you go through this book, you will do well to keep a few concepts in mind. As with any project, there will be a need to have a strong and reliable backdrop to support the additional effort required to operate the transformation you are undertaking. You'll soon realize that you're turning a page in your life, one of increased awareness. At times, you'll need to trust yourself to make it through to the end. Recognizing and applying the following concepts will ensure better use of your existing capabilities.

The Circle of Influence

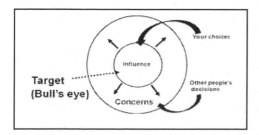

The Circle of Influence is a concept I consider to be of utmost importance. It provides a simple graphic which shows where your focus should be directed to attain Peak Performance.

AÏM FOR LIFE MASTERY™

Work on what you can change or affect and forget about what is totally dependent on other people's actions or decisions.

This concept was developed by Stephen Covey in his book *"The 7 Habits of Highly Effective People"*. The premise is that if we focus on our circle of INFLUENCE (the Bull's-eye), we reduce wasted energy, time and effort to meet everyday challenges. Conversely, if we let our aim wander into the circle of CONCERNS, we soon have less energy to take care of our own responsibilities. The moral of the story is to keep focused on your circle of influence and thus produce an expanding effect that reduces your circle of concerns. You gain more mastery over your life.

The Importance of Communications

Throughout this book, you will read about communication under its many different forms. The reason is quite simple.

> "The way we communicate with others and with ourselves ultimately determines the quality of our lives."
> — **Anthony Robbins,** Self-help author and success coach

According to research, success is due to roughly ten percent knowledge and over ninety percent communication skills. It makes sense to pay attention to how you transfer information, whether speaking to yourself, or to others.

One key sidebar to consider is the result of the work conducted at the University of Minnesota and reported by Ron Meiss. The research states that we basically communicate in the following four ways. In common circumstances, numbers reported are as follows:

Reading:	16 percent of the time
Writing:	9 percent
Speaking:	30 percent
Listening:	45 percent

PP = the right stuff, in the right amount, at the right time™

AÏM FOR LIFE MASTERY™

We receive communications more than we send.

According to these numbers, we should be listening a majority of the time. Yet we have a tendency to infringe on the very nature of communication's best practices! We have two ears and one mouth. If everything were equal, we should listen twice as much as we talk!

Word of Caution

The process of installing peak performance is a mental game with a specific purpose to make your effort more "**automatic**". It requires a uniform, consistent, and repeatable approach (premise of continuous improvement), and a systematic application of the recipe to develop new brain connections. It's a non-destructive process that obeys the law of repetition. Just as you would go to the gym to build muscle strength and agility, so it is for the development of your brain.

However, don't be too obsessive about the mental gym part, that period of mental workout that you commit to every day when you aim to be a peak performer! The subconscious brain is very smart and doesn't need continuous hours of repetition to get into motion. It only requires a gentle nudge in a regular, structured, and systematic way to keep it producing at peak capacity. Too much training can tire your brain. Make sure that your mental training is effective and productive by holding yourself to a maximum of two sessions per day. The optimal times are: 1) before bedtime, so that your brain continues to work while you sleep, and 2) when you wake up in the morning, as your brain is rested and less distracted. Under no circumstance should you practice more than twice per day, and for longer than 15 minutes at a time!

AÏM FOR LIFE MASTERY™

Recommendations for Maximum Effectiveness

<u>Breathe for Life</u>
All through this book, references are made to breathing as a key component of living and thinking.

You are encouraged to focus on your breathing as you scrutinize and absorb the various chapters in this book.

There's an old saying that the only thing you need is air. Anything else can be categorized as a "want". Do you agree? Of course, this refers to the immediacy of the air we require to stay alive.

You can live without food or water or many other things for different lengths of time. You will be uncomfortable but not in a do or die situation. But when it comes to air, it is critical and urgent. It's therefore recommended that the journey to peak performance start with learning how to breathe deeply to bring in maximum oxygen into your lungs. With plenty of oxygen, your body functions better, you think better, and on the whole, you feel better. Keep this in mind!

<u>Applying Force</u>
You must remember that the physical and the mental areas of our body are two distinct entities that operate differently but are intimately connected. The difference relates to the type of action that you take to train. For physical (muscle) training, the faster you move, or the heavier you lift, or the more the strain you put on the part of the body you want to develop, the more you will enable yourself to build speed, strength, and agility.

On the contrary, the development of your mental strength requires just the opposite. The less stress and strain you apply, the better the results. Brain development is optimized through a relaxed and quiet state of mind.

PP = the right stuff, in the right amount, at the right time™

AÏM FOR LIFE MASTERY™

Practice Away from the Performance Site

When we talk about the mental gym, we're talking about the place where you will want to conduct the exercises to build your mental capability. Your results will be amplified the greater distance you choose to practice from the site of performance. In the mental realm, you will want to minimize the impact of your surroundings while you work out mentally.

Therefore, be judicious in your choice of location where you do your mental gym. Make sure it is as remote as possible from your performance site so that you minimize the feelings associated (triggered) with the place where you work out. A clear mind, devoid of clouding by emotions associated with past performance, will be easier to reprogram for peak performance!

For example, take the football player who thinks he can't be as good as he could if he doesn't wear a certain T-shirt. So he puts on the T-shirt before going onto the field. There's really nothing to the shirt but the subconscious mental trigger it provides to put him into the performance state. You hear a lot about athletes' superstitions. A pair of socks, a certain shirt, a wristband, anything that triggers them into a superior state of performance is deemed to have a mysterious power. Most do not understand that the article actually creates a link to past peak performance, how they felt, how they performed, how they were "unstoppable".

Also, doing your mental practice away from the performance site ensures that you will have a tight connection with the imagined state, with minimal interference, and you'll be able to carry your preparation more easily into the arena of performance.

The PULL Concept

As you read this book, you will see references to the "PULL" concept. To help you understand and benefit fully from the use of this concept, I suggest that you think of a rope with which you're working. It's a rather large rope, bigger than your thumb in

---

diameter, and you have your two hands on it. It is linked to the activity you're leading. When you push the rope, you manage to advance but it takes quite an effort since the rope flexes and does not always translate your push into the right direction – it's hit or miss. However, if the rope pulls you, then it's only a matter of guiding the effort. It becomes easier to succeed at the task. Imagine the difference between towing a car with a rope, and pushing it with the rope. You can see already how much more effort would be required to push.

Throughout your daily routine, you'll have moments when you will push the rope - not a very easy task. At other times, the rope will pull you. The concept of the mental work described in this book is to develop the mental ability to create a pull on the rope, instead of having to push it.

I think that you'll agree that it's easier to guide the pull than to attempt to advance while pushing the rope. The best way I know to create that pull is to have a clear and compelling vision of where you want to go or be. Then the attraction of the destination acts to pull you in that direction. It reduces the effort required to get things done.

A Supporting Story

As you go through this book, you'll likely encounter moments when you'll have doubts about some of the precepts I'm advancing. Before you start discounting the process I'm about to disclose, I'd like to tell you about the story of one amazing person. Her name is Dr. Jill Bolte Taylor, Ph. D.

Dr. Taylor is a Harvard-trained neuro-anatomist, a brain scientist, who lived to recount the experience of a massive stroke she suffered at the age of 37. On December 10, 1996, she suffered the trauma of a massive brain haemorrhage in the left side of her brain. It left her without speech, memory, movement, mathematical ability and other faculties of recall. She wrote a book[4] about her eight year ordeal to recover her left brain abilities. She was recognized for her work in the May 2008 edition of Time Magazine as one of the 100 most influential people in the world.

Dr. Taylor recounts her recovery and how she followed and studied the steps her brain had to take to regain the faculties of speech, writing, memory, movement and recall. Because of her scientific knowledge, she was able to study the brain connections at work that allowed what seemed to be a miraculous recovery. She identified the process of how brain cells communicate through chemicals and brain circuitry to create new programs or mental models that help us deal automatically with our everyday challenges.

Her wish was that people would not have to live through a massive stroke to gain the insight she gained – an insight that can facilitate your journey to personal transformation toward peak performance (author's synopsis of Dr. Taylor's statements).

In a video accessible on YouTube[5], you can listen and view the explanations she shares on the accident she lived through. She explains how losing the cells that contained the memories of the past did not change her. The experience only eliminated the mental barriers she had built over her lifetime, barriers that prevented her from being her total self. You can watch other videos on the same site which further clarify the mechanisms that regulate our mental processes.

In essence, the reprogramming exercises discussed in this book are similar in impact to the impact of the stroke that Dr. Taylor describes. Contrary to Dr. Taylor's stroke, the exercises are non-destructive, but in the end, will transform the memories into

---

[4] Taylor, Dr. Jill Bolte, Ph.D. *My Stroke of Insight.* Viking Books. 2008
[5] YouTube.com - *How it feels to have a stroke.* 2009

cornerstones of performance, acting as springboards to new accomplishments aligned to the goals at which you are aiming.

The secret to success in your transformation, as Dr. Taylor suggests, is where you focus your attention. Your results will be proportional to the amount of focus you put into taking action to change your thinking habits. And it can be done through the capability of your brain to rewire itself under your conscious and focused guidance – mental programming for peak performance.

The Horse and The Rider

Before we go full steam ahead in, I would like to share how I view the concepts of our conscious and subconscious brains. First, let me tell you a story that involves horses.

When I was a youth working on the family farm, we used horses to do the heavy lifting. They were used to skid trees from the forest to the barn to make firewood in the Fall. They were the force that pulled the wagon when we cleaned out the barn and spread the manure on the fields. They were also used to mow the hay, gather it, and haul it to the barn during crop season. And for sure, we would have been working a lot harder if we didn't have them to pull loads of rocks, sand and dirt to build landscaping around the farm house.

With time, I came to know horses quite well. If you want horses to do what you want them to do, you need to guide them with reins, and sometimes pull hard to make them heed your commands. The horses (like the subconscious brain) want to go their habitual way, and the driver (RIDER) keeps them on the path to completion of the task. Thus, just like the horse and the rider, the subconscious brain tends to go where it's used to going, and the conscious brain rationalizes and logically drives us to do the appropriate thing at the right time.

AÏM FOR LIFE MASTERY™

So the story goes like this. One summer, while gathering hay in the field, we were loading up with my brother and grandfather and we hit a wasps' nest. For those of you who know about horses, you can imagine that they were spooked. Being in the middle of the field, the horses were not tied. The reins were just resting on the rack.

Picture this. There was a little brook running across the farm which practically dried up in the summer months. However, we still needed a bridge to cross it. Beyond the bridge was a fence with a wooden gate for controlled access to the field. From there, a path went winding to the barn through the cow pasture.

When the horses were spooked by the wasps, they did not care that they were hitched to the hay wagon. They started running toward their usual destination, the barn. Of course, the field was not a paved road! Progressively, as the horses ran, pulling the wagon over the rough terrain, the wagon started coming apart! Now they had reached the bridge. Think they lined up properly to cross? Not a chance! So, crossing the bridge, a few more planks and pieces flew off, from the bridge and from the wagon. Imagine that the gate was immediately on the other side of the bridge and you can already see disaster increasing. The poor horses were now in full flight. Bang! Right through the gate they went, pulling a post and destroying the gate.

Their wild ride finally ended when they got to the barn where they usually came to rest. It was devastating to watch all that happening at the time. We had to bring in the crop, and our main hauling wagon was practically destroyed. And that's not even counting the work it took to repair the bridge, the gate and the hay frame for the wagon.

Today, as I think back to that episode, it reminds me of how our subconscious brain works, just like the horses. If it is spooked by something we're afraid of, or don't know about, we have a knee jerk reaction. We start running without thinking too much. We take action that seems at times totally stupid. We don't even notice what is going on around us. Our actions are driven by the automatic responses based on past experiences. And we usually don't assess or evaluate before taking off (figuratively) to protect ourselves.

As you read through this book, keep this concept in mind. To succeed, you need to learn to be a good RIDER and guide your HORSE (subconscious brain) to do what you want it to do. The techniques we'll examine together are meant to help you gain mastery of your horse (the subconscious brain) by teaching it to respond appropriately and effectively in challenging times – to create peak performance.

Key Points to Remember

- As you read, remember to take a step back and be objective; ask yourself how you can use these concepts and ideas to increase your results.

- The title is meant to make you shoot for more than the ordinary automatic.

- This book is a way to share years of experience in creating peak performance – please pay attention and seek to grab at least one technique or trick to make your life easier.

- You are encouraged to read all the way through. You never know when the personal discovery of a closely guarded secret can propel you to a significant personal transformation.

- Refer to the roadmap when you feel lost. Make sure you know what step you have reached in your journey to peak performance.

AÏM FOR LIFE MASTERY™

- In simple terms, this book is about seeking to reduce effort and to increase results while reducing stress – effort-less effectiveness.

- You have lived your life up to now. Surely you have all it takes to make it a success in the future. This is nothing new. Just remember the process makes all the difference. This book provides a structured approach to create peak performance.

- We are continuously creating new thinking pathways (being programmed and reprogrammed). Why not learn how to use this natural ability and do it consciously so that you can reach for peak performance on a routine basis?

- Along the way, Peak Performance will be helped if you keep in mind:
  - the Circle of Influence – focus on what you can control
  - the importance of communicating properly
  - the notion of "**automatic**"
  - breathing for life; make sure you fill yourself with oxygen
  - physically, you need more effort to produce impact
  - mentally, the less you strain, the more you gain
  - the PULL concept: it is easier to pull than to push on a rope.

- There are countless illustrations of the mind's power and what it can do; remember Dr. Jill Bolte Taylor and her journey to complete recovery from a massive stroke.

- When considering most of the concepts and ideas you encounter, keep in mind the story of the horse and the rider. Your subconscious brain is like the horse – it goes where it bloody well pleases. YOU as the rider (your conscious brain) must take the reins and guide the horse where you want it to go. This takes practice and time.

AÏM FOR LIFE MASTERY™

PART II – BUILDING THE FOUNDATION

STAYING ON TRACK...

AÏM FOR LIFE MASTERY™

Fundamentals of AÏM

Before I share the recipe for installing peak performance, I want to make sure that we're on the same page. If you're to be guided effectively by my message, it's important that we speak the same language, use the same terminology.

You might have read about this subject, heard experts in the field talk about it, or exchanged opinions on performance with other people. Mastery is the key to success in establishing "**automatic**" responses that will support your journey to peak performance.

I define my program as AÏM – the keys to life mastery. It's a somewhat simple acronym but heavy with significance:

A – stands for <u>awareness </u>(having the knowledge that something exists)

I – <u>internalize</u> the awareness (put the fact in your knowledge bag for future use)

I – <u>integrate</u> the awareness into your routine (use the knowledge to deliver in an effort-less way). It's represented by the second dot on the "i" as the author's perspective of the integrated sense of the framework; internalizing and integrating are two sides of one activity to implement peak performance. One does not go without the other.

M - <u>mastery</u> gained through continuous practice (repeat the application of the knowledge) so it becomes "**automatic**" when challenges appear.

I chose this acronym to summarize the important steps you must take to gain mastery and produce Peak Performance.

AÏM FOR LIFE MASTERY™

There's another reason. I think you'll agree that "If you don`t aim, you will seldom hit it". I believe that mastery is not an accident. It is the direct result of a focused and sustained action to attain an automatic response. Ask any high level athlete. He or she will tell you that their skill is the result of countless hours of dedicated practice. The process is simple, but it's hard work, and it takes patience and perseverance. Therefore, **AïM** is meant to call upon your will to excel!

At this point, I believe it's important to underline the main functions of the brain.

I won't burden you with the technicalities of how your brain works but rather talk about the notional functioning of the brain. Let's look at two parts of interest, the conscious and the subconscious brains.

The subconscious brain (limbic or autonomous system) controls our <u>instinct</u>. It drives the autonomous body functions such as digestion, blood circulation, breathing, healing, and fighting bacteria and germs without our conscious knowledge. It's also the location of automatic reactions based on our beliefs. It would seem that this part of the brain is much more powerful than the conscious part. It sounds like it would be very beneficial to learn how to use the subconscious part of our brain more readily!

The conscious brain is where our knowledge is stored. What we've learned as we grew up, our life experiences, the skills we developed by doing things. All are deposited in memory and can be tapped at the right time to support our conscious thinking. It's also the location of our ability to see, hear, taste, feel a touch, learn and create new concepts, new understandings.

The goal of creating <u>mastery</u> is to create automatic responses to situations by a combination of recognition, established mental models, and timely application of "automatic" responses that reduce effort and ensure focused results. However, before the response becomes automatic, there has to be a process to transfer the information or concept from the conscious to the subconscious brain.

In the following pages, you will read about a technique to increase the ability you already have to create new mental pathways that will enable you to be a peak performer.

Awareness Training

The first letter of **AïM** is A, and it stands for <u>awareness</u>.

In the English Thesaurus, awareness has many definitions. They include: consciousness, wakefulness, responsiveness, recognition, discernment, perception, grasp, familiarity.

When you read these words, you will realize that awareness simply means taking note of the present, and assessing it in a way that will provide a sound basis for action. Too often, we miss cues passing by in the normal course of the day because we're not fully sharp mentally, or lack full recognition of the facts. This is simply because our recognition patterns are not alert. At other times, we miss a cue - verbal, visual or otherwise - because we more or less float through the moment in time, oblivious to our surroundings.

I won't go as far as to say that we are sleeping at the wheel, but rather, that our level of awareness is low in certain circumstances! Many factors come into play. It could be a lack of sleep, momentary distraction, dehydration due to lack of fluids, or not enough vitamins or….. The reasons are varied. What's important is to train our brain to recognize cues and signals that trigger our awareness.

AÏM FOR LIFE MASTERY™

Internalizing the Discovery

In the word **AïM,** there are two "i"s. The first symbolizes the word "internalize".

Over the many programs I've delivered, I have learned that before anything can happen, you must store the new awareness into your bag of tricks. Otherwise, it will be hit or miss as far as using it.

For example, considering a relationship between two people, one can suddenly recognize that certain words produce a certain level of response. Imagine the cap on the toothpaste tube. Men have a tendency to leave the cap off, and that drives women up the wall! Or leaving the toilet seat up after use!!! With time, the predictability of the response is 100 percent. Now, if a man is so unaware that he disregards the emotional fit his spouse goes into every time the cap or the seat is not in place, he simply lacks awareness. But once he realizes the impact his lack of awareness has on his relationship, he can store this realization, and make an effort to correct his omission. He is now internalizing the awareness. In his head, a sudden reflection has shown the benefit of putting the seat down or putting the cap on – no more ranting or raving from his spouse!!!

By recognizing and assessing the situation, and rationally concluding the benefit of the action, a person internalizes the awareness and can now act upon it.

Integrating into the Routine

In the word **AïM**, the second "i" stands for "integrate". It's not sufficient to internalize the awareness. We must make the awareness part of our daily thinking. Once internalized, the awareness is present, but it doesn't serve a purpose unless it's put into action.

For example, my spouse has been telling me for a long time to call her if I'm going to be late. I know and understand why she wishes to be informed. I have internalized her wish. However, I have not fully integrated that knowledge. Sometimes, I forget about the desired phone call and it creates a bit of discomfort in the relationship. That's not peak performance since it leads to unnecessary reminders and discussions that do not add value. I should know better and integrate!

Results only happen once the action to integrate is taken.

It's a challenge you must resolve to face. As with anything else, without focus and sustained attention, the results will be hard to come by. To integrate the new awareness, it will be necessary to keep the process in mind. Every time you have a proverbial "aha", you will want to do a bit of mental planning. Perhaps making a note with the intention to use it will help to internalize it. In sequence, the third step will follow. You will want to make sure that, not only do you now realize the new awareness and want to carry it with you, but you intentionally want to use it to get better – seeking Peak Performance.

Repeating the process for every new awareness will help establish a habit of recognition which, in time, will become automatic. The ability to internalize and integrate will become second nature. Peak Performance will become part of your life!

AÏM FOR LIFE MASTERY™

Developing Mastery

The last letter of **AïM** stands for MASTERY.

After gaining awareness of a concept or technique or skill, after working diligently to internalize this tool in your bag of tricks, and integrating the new capability consciously into your routine, the last step is to bring it to second nature (or on **automatic**), a way of dealing with the new awareness on a continuous basis.

As for any skill or activity we master through practice, the new awareness needs to be practiced to become permanently engraved into a habit, the habit of mastery.

> "Any idea, plan, or purpose may be placed in the mind through repetition of thought."
> — **Napoleon Hill,** Lecturer and author of books on achieving success

I think here of Gandhi's words: "Keep my words positive, they become my behaviours. Keep my behaviours positive, they become my habits. Keep my habits positive, they become my beliefs. Keep my beliefs positive, they become my destiny." Looking at that quote, we get a sense of the progression which ultimately describes the practice required to reach the "destiny" we desire. As Einstein once said, "The best way to determine our future is to create it."

Creating a desired future requires consistency, determination, focus, perseverance and persistence, courage and dedication. You owe it to yourself to make it as easy as possible! Life is hard enough as it is. Most of the time, no one will strive to make it easy for you. Makes sense, doesn't it?

People have to take care of their own lives first. Only philanthropists will come out specifically to support you. Most

AÏM FOR LIFE MASTERY™

people around you have their hands full living their own lives. Putting effort into developing **M**astery will ensure that the potential and possibilities for optimal results will raise your performance to a level beyond what you would have ever believed achievable!

When you decide to develop **M**astery, you will confirm Peak Performance as a part of your daily routine, and you will create the **PULL** that will take you toward an "effort-less" achievement of your life goals.

AÏM FOR LIFE MASTERY™

Peak Performance Defined

For the sake of simplicity and common understanding, let me first explain how I view peak performance.

I'm sure you've read, heard or been exposed to a number of definitions on the subject. For the purpose of this guide, I want you to think about peak performance in very simple terms.

> "In order to get the best result with the least effort, it pays to use the K.I.S.S. Principle (keep it super simple)".
> - **Dan Blais,** friend and business colleague

I want you to imagine that peak performance is like a well-balanced recipe. Too much salt will waste a perfectly delicious meal. Similarly, too much effort to be perfect will wear you down and may, in the end, be contrary to attaining your highest level of achievement.

I want you to have a relaxed perspective when considering peak performance.

Over the years, experience has taught me that peak performance is not "the pedal to the metal". Contrary to conventional wisdom, peak performance does not rely on 100% effort all of the time. Instead, my experience has demonstrated just the opposite.

Let's look at an everyday situation which illustrates the concept.

You likely drive a car most every day. Unless you are a race car driver, you seldom have the pedal to the metal. But chances are that you've had a close call on the road at one point in time. Because you were in the moment, your awareness allowed you to use your driving skills to the max: you steered, maybe braked, and avoided an accident, without losing control, without landing in the ditch, without even thinking about it.

Everything happened perfectly to deal with the situation. You were in peak performance – the right stuff, in the right amount, at exactly the right time. It was an automatic response. And that's what you want to create for all important situations. You want to implement a mental program that allows you to make use of your acquired knowledge and skills in a way that produces the best possible results with minimal effort.

So I propose to you the following definition for peak performance:

The right stuff, in the right amount, at the right time™

I can't help but think about Kenny Rogers' song *The* Gambler when I think of peak performance. Words go as follows: "You've got to know when to hold 'em, know when to fold 'em, know when to walk away, know when to run...". The analogy is linked to the action. Peak Performance is about minimum effort and maximum results. And so goes my definition.

Therefore, for the sake of having a common understanding of Peak Performance, I will explain what I mean through the following diagram. Life is a path from A to B. The straight line is the optimum

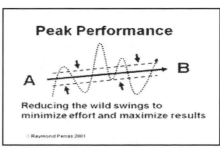

Peak Performance

Reducing the wild swings to minimize effort and maximize results

travel, but we know life is not that way. There are moments of deviation that take us off course. Often, we need to rectify our direction in order to progress to the goal. Applying the Peak Performance process reduces the costly curves and minimizes wasted effort.

AÏM FOR LIFE MASTERY™

Peak Performance, in my perspective, is based on the following three pillars – the stuff, the amount, and the timing. While reading and reflecting on the ideas in this book, I want you to remember this definition and the suggestions offered for effective action. In simple terms, Peak Performance is the process by which you minimize effort while increasing your results.

The Right Stuff

I must confess that I'm a stickler for simplicity. What's important to me is that you understand the concept so that you can apply the formula, and gain a higher level of awareness of what you can really do.

In this vein, for the first pillar of peak performance, I have coined THE RIGHT STUFF to mean all the knowledge, experiences, abilities, skills and expertise you've developed and stored over your life. After all, you didn't get to where you are now by magic! Your efforts to learn, assess, evaluate, to think and rethink, to accept, absorb, choose, apply, all have led you to be able to deal with situations in your everyday life. You're probably pretty good at dealing with issues or obstacles that appear in your daily situations.

All those moments where you've used your stored capabilities have made you strong. You have what it takes to design and lead a good life. There's just one thing, sometimes, you get distracted, and when a challenge presents itself, you don't always deal with it the way you should. These are moments when you don't make use of THE RIGHT STUFF! You let things happen, instead of making them happen. Sometimes, the results are not quite what you desired.

Only later, when hindsight sets in, you realize that you missed the boat. You could have done something different if you had been "all there". In a word, you could have chosen a different action based on your stored knowledge.

AÏM FOR LIFE MASTERY™

Let me give an example. A couple of friends are waiting at the movie theatre to buy tickets; there's a long line up. Two people arrive from the other direction and cut into the front of the line. It seems that nobody noticed, but our two subjects are miffed by the whole thing. They voice a couple of expletives toward the obnoxious pair. A verbal sparring match ensues. Threats are made. Everyone around, including families with young children are upset. A lot of commotion could have been avoided if either of the parties had been more aware of the situation and acted with more courtesy.

Both sides reacted on "automatic", one expressing anger, while the other responded with total disrespect. They were let down by their "automatic". There was a result all right, but it was not beneficial to anyone. That's when the proverbial "Oh no!" comes to the fore and an observer of the situation cannot help but wonder what would have happened if only they had cared more for the people around them.

Perhaps it sounds like an over-simplification, but in short, that's basically the root cause of the misstep: they sure didn't use the right stuff!!!

Once you start to realize and become aware that you must be more selective in applying actions to your situation, you raise the quality of your results through the first pillar of Peak Performance – THE RIGHT STUFF.

In The Right Amount

It's essential to have the right amount if you want to have a successful recipe.

Take baking a cake as an example. Forget or modify the recipe by just one ingredient, and you might have a big flop. Equally

AÏM FOR LIFE MASTERY™

important is the second pillar for peak performance – THE RIGHT AMOUNT. Ingredients are critical, but the amount is crucial. If the recipe calls for a pinch of salt and you mistakenly add a tablespoon, just imagine the taste of the cake. Going back to the theatre line up example, if the people who became angry at those who were cutting in chose to either maintain their composure or choose a more subtle way of expressing their view, the impact would have been quite different.

It makes me think of the time when I was young and adventurous. We kids in the family decided to make apple pies. We did everything right except that we mistook the salt for sugar – looked the same, white, granular. So proud we were of our pies. We cooked them and excitedly waited for dessert time to eat one. Never tasted such a bad apple pie! Imagine the salty taste plus the ice cream on top. Yuck!!!!!

In keeping with this simple explanation, THE RIGHT AMOUNT is simply a measured dose of whatever skill, experience, knowledge, ability, or expertise you can apply in any given circumstance. Too much and you overwhelm people around you, or conversely, you over-extend yourself uselessly and waste energy. Worse yet, you can look like a fool for over-reacting and applying the proverbial hammer to kill the ant. Too much of a good thing is a bad thing. At least, that's what I was taught in school.

Again, I allude to the awareness required to measure our effort to achieve peak performance in action. In my evaluation of return on investment (ROI or effort to produce a result), I truly believe that we should be mindful of applying an effort that is equal to the demand, no more, no less. Life is too short to waste energy. We should save it so that we have some left for other priorities!

This reminds me of a client who complained about his boss always telling him, "You're trying too hard". He was totally confused by the comment. He worked hard to meet goals and produce expected results. His performance was recognized as more than average. But he felt that the comment from his boss hinted at relaxing despite being a stickler for quality and timely results. A real mixed message. With a little bit of introspection through questioning, we focused on his personal view of the situation. He soon realized that in his desire to meet expectations, he was letting stress blur his awareness. At times, he was spinning his wheels even though he had the ability, capacity, and competency to deliver excellent work. He was trying too hard, and that defeated his purpose. We implemented a breathing exercise to be used every morning before going to work. It was magical. In a week, my client felt relaxed and found out how much more he could accomplished with less effort. He had learned to apply the **RIGHT AMOUNT**.

To my way of thinking, life is much more pleasant when we don't feel worn out at the end of the day! THE RIGHT AMOUNT goes a long way to support this approach. It provides the second pillar to produce peak performance. For those who seek to get more out of life, I think this one's a keeper.

At The Right Time

The first two pillars of peak performance ensure that we have the right ingredients in the recipe, and the right amount to produce the desired result. The third pillar – **THE RIGHT TIME** - is no less important. If we get back to the cake analogy, we can have the right ingredients and measure the right amount, but, what if what is required is not a cake but a good old bowl of soup? Cake is good, but it won't be well received if it's offered at the wrong time. You get the point.

The third pillar to ensure peak performance is also a critical component of a systematic approach to produce optimal results.

AÏM FOR LIFE MASTERY™

If we go back to the driving example, I'm sure that you can grasp right away the synergy of time with stuff and amount. Say you anticipate too much as you are faced with the road condition. You will likely over-steer or brake too early, and end up in a precarious spot. The same applies if you are too late in reacting to the situation. You are more than likely to be unable to avoid a collision. Timing is indeed everything. But that third pillar is difficult to apply if your awareness is at a low level. Think **right time** and you will greatly increase your chances for success when facing challenges.

A lot has been written and said about time, but in my opinion, it's too often dealt with in isolation. The right stuff, the right amount, and the right time, the three pillars of peak performance must be sequenced and timed to create a framework that guides the effort to a positive and optimal conclusion. It is said that timing is everything - in business, investment, sports, games, relationships, even unwanted events. It seems that the prize goes to the ones who have the right "timing". Consequently, the third pillar of peak performance must be considered as being even more important than the other two.

I remember many years ago as I was building my career as an engineer. In those days, housing prices were increasing due to the bursting economy in Western Canada. Like many of my peers, I looked to increase my assets by buying a house when I moved to Edmonton. I used the right stuff in the right amount; I bought a house that fitted my income. However, the timing was wrong. Eight years later, when I moved back East, the house was worth about nine percent less than the original price. You could say the economy did me in, but the fact was that timing was not the best. If I had moved to Eastern Canada three years sooner as a few of my peers did, I would have realized a 30 percent profit.

AÏM FOR LIFE MASTERY™

In conclusion, this definition may not jive with your understanding of the world around you, but I assure you, that if you respect the premise of **THE RIGHT STUFF, IN THE RIGHT AMOUNT, AT THE RIGHT TIME**™, you will raise your performance to unexpected levels.

The reason is simple. Paying attention to stuff, amount, and time makes you aware of every situation, and directly impacts how you handle it. It raises your focus and increases your power of concentration. It allows you to dip into your bag of knowledge, skills, abilities and insights in a way that is in tune with the circumstances. You minimize waste of energy, psychological, emotional, physical, and even spiritual. In doing so, you will make more effective use of your skills, knowledge, experience, and capabilities to accomplish what you set out to do. You will be a PEAK PERFORMER.

Meet a REAL Peak Performer

I want to share with you the story of a client who has become a REAL peak performer. Names have been changed to preserve anonymity.

Six years ago, a man was referred to me by a coaching client. Marty was a territory salesman for a flooring company. He was looking to improve his public speaking skills in order to deliver his sales pitch more effectively. As I am an Able Toastmaster, my referring client thought I could help Marty.

As usual in my practice, I applied the Peak Performance process: vision, mission, values, goals, roles, procedures and relationships. I worked with him to define what he focused on to establish his motivation. Everything fitted well with my structured and systematic approach. However, Marty had personal issues. One was his relationship with Rachel who was not aligned with his life vision. To his credit, Marty followed the coaching, ended that relationship, adopted a peak performance attitude and got to work. Over time, I provided insight and guidance for a number of challenges in his business including problem personnel and his own ambitions to reach his full potential. Many milestones were reached, and progressively, Marty learned to become a master at living his life. He also got good at public speaking!

Today, married to a wonderful woman who walks with him every step of the way, he has a beautiful family with two kids, has achieved regional sales manager in his company, has gained tremendous confidence in his experience and abilities, and has even lost weight and become a long distance runner. In the spring of 2011, Marty ran a half marathon and was overjoyed with his performance.

All along his journey, I have watched Marty get better and better as he practiced, practiced, practiced and became a master of his life. He now has defined his ultimate vision, to be his own boss and run a real estate investment business. He already has a number of properties under his ownership, and both he and his wife look to a wonderful and happy life as owners and managers of their assets.

To me, Marty is the full complement of what a peak performer is. He has learned the process and applies it by always observing **the right stuff, in the right amount, at the right time**™ through his awareness, his ability to internalize and integrate, and respecting the key to mastery, practice, practice, practice.

NOW, THAT'S PEAK PERFORMANCE!

AÏM FOR LIFE MASTERY™

Aligning Your Compass

Before setting sail, a ship usually has to have a set direction. Otherwise, as performance guru and well-known author Denis Waitley[6] says, "… if you don't know where you're going, you're on the road to nowhere." Much planning and allocation of resources can be all for nothing!

> "Many can argue that reality is as it is, but my experience is that the opposite is exactly true, reality is ours for the making."
> — **Asara Lovejoy**, Human potential author and coach

In peak performance, the first step is to determine the direction in which the effort will be applied. It is the one most crucial decision to minimize waste. Clarity of purpose leads to clarity of action. The key is to be certain of your goal by asking the question "where do I want to be at a certain time?" You'll want to describe the place you want to reach, and define the time you will take to make the result happen. Begin with the end in mind.

Over the many years of managing projects, developing plans for my employers, or providing support to organizations seeking to use resources effectively, I've developed the deep conviction that this step requires imagination. You might say "no one can predict the future". But, as strange as it might seem, it's this very capability that ensures effective application of effort. I agree that change will inevitably happen. But if you start with a clear idea of where you want to be, you will act in a way that will raise the possibility of hitting the mark.

---

[6] Waitley, Denis. *The Psychology of Winning*, Audio-cassette program, Nightingale-Conant, 1990

AÏM FOR LIFE MASTERY™

The Power of Vision

How often have you seen someone achieve unexpected results? How many times have you observed successful people and wished you had their luck? Or have you ever wondered how the rich and famous become that way? If you look more closely, every one of these remarkable results are linked to a clear vision of the future. Just think how John F. Kennedy launched the USA into an exploration project that ended with Neil Armstrong stepping on the surface of the moon July 21, 1969. He publicly announced his vision that a man would set foot on the moon by the end of the sixties; and the rest is history.

Nothing happens until it has first been imagined. Think of your own experience. Have you ever ended up in an exotic place without having first dreamed of being there, making plans, saving money, organizing the details so that everything happened to allow you to achieve that dream? Too often, we end up in a place where we don't really want to be. Too often also, we forget that we drew our own lot through our own thinking, or imagining. Whatever we think about, we bring into our own reality. Whether you think you want, or you don't want, the result is the same. As Waitley would say, "You get what you set."

Thinking on the positive side, let's imagine that a desired result will happen if we imagine it clearly. There is no guarantee. But if we make use of the **PULL** concept, it will be easier to work toward what we want. It will establish a constant pull on you toward the clearly defined vision of the future you have crafted. You will need much less energy to be pulled than it would take to push toward the goal. That's what a vision will do for you. It will draw you, attract you, move you to action, and keep you focused on what is required to reach it.

Let me give you an example of my own journey. Many years ago, I developed the desire to work with athletes at the professional level. I had a vision of helping them increase their performance by

---

integrating mental preparation into their professional practice. It took over ten years of continuous effort working with the University of Ottawa football program before I got my break. In 2000, we won the national championship and the head coach established himself through that success. He soon landed a job in the Canadian Football League. When he called me to work with one of his athletes, my dream came true. But if I had not entertained the vision of that day, I would not have worked with university athletes for as long as I did to get there. After all, my work with the university football program was all volunteer work.

Thus, it's necessary to have a clear vision if you want to minimize your effort and raise the likelihood that you will reach your set goal. When one thinks calmly about life, I think we would all agree that it's worth looking for ways to reduce the effort it takes to live. Why not make it a game, and practice drafting a vision for all goals or objectives that merit your attention? It's possible that you will get good at creating the pull that a vision creates. It will make your life that much easier to live. It will make you a peak performer!

Evidently, to create a pull, your vision needs to be compelling. It will reach deep down inside you and stir up a drive that allows you to charge toward the desired goal, no matter what obstacle lies in front of you. For that to be real, you'll want to tap into your best memories and experiences to bring up what really turns you on.

It's the qualities of past events that will direct you to a choice of descriptors that make you swell with a deep emotion. Remember that motivation is from within. No one knows as well as you do what makes you burn with an overwhelming desire to succeed.

If this exercise seems foreign for you, I've provided a few pointers and a sample vision in Appendix 1. You can use the following guidelines to initiate your thinking toward your desired vision of the future. Review the guidelines and follow the directions to facilitate the creation of a compelling vision for yourself.

Basic Rules for Vision Building

In my work with numerous clients, and learning by experience, a compelling vision must be written in a certain way to ensure that it's effective. I call it the **3P Rule of Vision Building**©. If your vision is to be the most powerful it can be, it must reach your subconscious brain and avoid creating automatic barriers – words that trigger your subconscious mind into denial.

You must remember that self-talk is very powerful, and is the essence of programming your mind. You do it continually when talking to yourself. You must therefore be careful to use words that will propel you, as opposed to grounding you in negativity.

Another consideration when writing your vision is to make it just out of reach, so that it stretches you, but is not completely out of sight. Taking that approach allows you to stay focused on it.

People who have done the research suggest that five to ten years into the future should be selected. Some of the reasons for that are clear. Down the road and far enough, anything is possible but too close and right away, you will think of reasons why it can't be done. A few years ahead gives you the time to take action, so no problem if it seems to be a stretch. Also, putting the vision far enough into the future will allow you to think in terms of letting your vision flesh out, and be enriched by changing reality.

The 3P Rule© consists of three elements that you should consider when defining your vision. Personal. Present. Positive.

First, the vision statement must be **personal** to be effective. Wishing that someone else will modify a certain behaviour will seldom work, or at least, produce the desired result in the expected timeframe. We can only change ourselves. Suffice it to say that any action statement should begin with "I" and the object of the action should also be "I". The objective is to change your behaviour for the better, and to drive yourself to do what is required to reach the goal you have in mind.

For example, a vision statement that works for me is "I am confident that I can face the challenge given by this contractual demand". Once in a while, I'm asked to take on work that stretches my knowledge and abilities to perform in a way that will meet the client's needs. By telling myself that I can succeed, I remove the doubt that could prevent me from being creative, and find the adequate solution to the challenge at hand.

Last year, one of my clients requested a national opinion survey of its thousands of employees on corporate statements for a people management philosophy and a leadership commitment. At first, this seemed a daunting task. However, I quickly cast my look at the potential end product and soon got an idea of how to bring it about. Looking ahead and visioning that end product allowed me to tap my experience and expertise to design a method that would produce the desired result.

Second, we must make very sure that we drive our subconscious brain to the desired goal. As your subconscious doesn't know the difference between what is imagined and what is real, you can use this to create thoughts that appear to have already happened.

Thus **present** is the second element of your vision exercise. This basically causes your subconscious brain to be drawn to the reality you sow in your mind. It may not have arrived yet, but if you want your subconscious brain to pull you to the vision, you will want to sow the idea of the desired future as if it had already happened. In essence, you fool your subconscious brain into seeking the desired result, and in doing so, create an internal drive toward the vision.

AÏM FOR LIFE MASTERY™

Third, your vision statement should be built with **positive words**. Positive action results from having positive thoughts. For example, try this. To get the maximum result when trying to quit smoking, use the qualifier "I am a non-smoker". This will be more effective than "I don't smoke".

Your brain will have a tendency to latch on to the action word "smoke" and discard the word "don't". For that reason, every word used should depict a positive action so that your subconscious brain is fed the right stuff. In that sense, the subconscious brain is like a garden. It grows whatever thoughts (seeds) you have sown. Just like a garden grows beautiful flowers if good seeds are planted, so does your brain produce good thinking from positive thoughts. Negative thoughts produce negative thinking. Stay away from planting bad seeds!

At this point, you're probably wondering if this really works.

Let me give you a personal example.

Many years ago, I had seen pictures of the Pyramids in Egypt. I was fascinated by the mysteries surrounding that wonder of the world. I caressed the dream of seeing them, walking around, exploring, finding out for myself about these miracles of ancient construction (it was the engineer in me!!).

The dream was there. The thought would recur once in a while, and I even dreamed about the Pyramids, in all their intricate details, complete with camels walking around the Sphinx.

Then in 1988, as if fate had arranged for the dream to come true, I had an invitation from friends who had recently been posted in Cairo, Egypt, to go and visit with them. I planned the trip and flew from Canada to Paris. Then I was on a plane to Cairo, where I was welcomed with open arms. Not only did my friends introduce me to Egypt, but having a personal chauffeur as part of their benefits, I was provided with a personal guide to visit the Great

---

AÏM FOR LIFE MASTERY™

Pyramids immediately West of Cairo, travel up the Nile to Saqqara to see the Step Pyramid of Djoser, and see the sacred bulls' tombs. I also had the privilege of visiting Alexandria on the north edge of Egypt where the Nile meets the South Mediterranean Sea. I even got to see the famous Cairo market and bought souvenirs which I enjoy to this day.

It was spectacular proof to me that the power of vision worked.

Stop and think for a moment about your own life. Isn't this the way everything happens to you? Before you go to a restaurant, you think about what you would like to eat, and then you develop a desire to eat that food. If you want to have fun doing a hobby or meeting friends or…. you first think about it in a positive way, see yourself enjoying it, as if it had already happened. Then you develop a desire to take action, and do it. If the desire is lukewarm, you might very well forego the event because it did not **PULL** you strongly enough.

Events that you visualize and perceive as desirable will give you the motivation necessary to overcome all barriers in order to experience them. It's really that simple.

Building a vision of the future, creating a strong pull toward a desired goal, taking positive and effective action to make sure we reach the target, those things happen all the time. We're just not aware of the process that's going on in our heads and in our hearts. Writing a compelling and powerful vision is essentially becoming aware of the power you have to shape your own destiny, and taking action to ensure you get what you are aiming for.

> It is all very well to copy what you see, but it is better to draw what you see in your mind …. Then your memory and imagination are freed from the tyranny imposed by nature.
> Edgar Degas

AÏM FOR LIFE MASTERY™

There's no mystery, just the innate capability we all have to shape our future in a wilful manner. Ultimately, the choice is ours. Everyone can shape what will happen in the future, if we really want!

In the end, it's a matter of setting your compass so that whether it's sunny, raining, or stormy (life resembles that sometimes), your compass will always point to True North, and you will never get lost in the trials and tribulations that inevitably will come to distract you from the direction in which you want to go. A powerful and compelling vision will act as a beacon to help you keep your ship on course, and minimize the costly detours (curves) that are present when you are not clear enough on where you want to go.

Perhaps it would be useful to talk a little about the daunting task that creating a vision of the future might seem for you. You might say, "I don't really know where I want to be in five to ten years".

I think that like many of us, you're just letting your fear of the unknown grip you. What if I don't get it done? What if something happens that torpedoes my vision, and makes it impossible? What if I change my mind, and don't want to go there anymore?

Well, that's the reason why it's a five to ten year vision!

There's plenty of time to adjust, to rectify, or to just plain turn back. The important thing about a vision is not to lock you into a path, but rather, to unleash the energy that you possess to charge toward your destiny. Someone once said, "If you don't aim, you will seldom hit". And the main reason we don't hit is that we often direct our energy willy-nilly, with no specific goal in mind. To my way of thinking, that's called waste. And life is too short to waste it. You must start thinking in terms of maximizing your efforts to produce the desired results.

AÏM FOR LIFE MASTERY™

Believe and You Shall See

It's incredible how the power of belief (and the resulting effect and impact that it has on our actions) ultimately leads to the desired results. It's critical to set the course and aim for the goal, but if the drive is not there, you're essentially treading water!

For example, in 1986, I wanted to be part of a relay race from Jasper to Banff, Alberta, Canada, a 290-kilometre run. I did run the odd 5 km or 10 km race before but this meant two relays of 15 to 25 km in a two-day period on mountainous roads. The desire to be part of that experience drove me to train and get physically and mentally ready for the race. On the weekend of the race, I raced my best times and felt so proud of doing what I had committed to do. I believed I could do it, and I did!

As we've seen, focus is the primary source of motivation. Focus your attention on a desired state, and you will progressively develop deep down motivation to move toward that state. It's the Law of Attraction at work. However, as much as you wish to move, movement will only be significant if the belief in the reward of the movement will provide pleasure. Belief builds by repeated imagination of the benefit. As much as it can sound unbelievable, it's that simple. Belief grows proportionately to the amount of focus you put on the benefit of the desired outcome.

It's somewhat of a chicken and egg concept. You'll have desire and motivation if you imagine the outcome. If you imagine the outcome, you allow stronger and deeper focus. Deeper focus creates the desire (motivation to move in order to produce the benefit). The more you practice seeing, the more you develop belief. The more your belief grows, the more you're driven to act in order to produce the result. And the more you act, the more you create the concrete expression of the desire, bringing about the possibility to see the end play.

AÏM FOR LIFE MASTERY™

Comprehensive and Inspiring

As for anything we bring into our view and develop a liking or even a love for, your vision will become compelling only if it is "comprehensive" and "inspiring".

<u>Comprehensive</u>

Let me define "comprehensive". When you define your vision, you should remember that, as a human being, you are a holistic entity. You are a physical, emotional, mental, and psychological being. You carry all perspectives together, all in one basket – social, community, financial, family, well-being, professional, physical, emotional, relationships, knowledge, experience, etc.

As an individual with all those angles to take into account, it pays to take some time and brainstorm what your vision is going to be.

It becomes very clear that if you're to design a powerful vision, you should include details from all of these aspects so that you can create balance in your effort. Otherwise, you might do well at first, but soon, you'll find that you are off-balance, with a distinct feeling of discomfort. It may show up as stress that you can't explain.

The details you include should clearly and thoroughly define what you are aiming for, so that you provide guidance to your subconscious brain – create the PULL as opposed to having to PUSH to get where you want to go.

<u>Inspiring</u>

As we've seen previously, even if you have the best guidance system in place, you won't be moved to the degree you're seeking by words that just plain leave you cold. Your vision statement should use words that turn your crank, empower you to

AÏM FOR LIFE MASTERY™

rise to be the best, put you into a state of emotion that supports the drive to the prize.

Here's something that really works for me. When I want to generate maximum motivation in any given moment, I use words like "powerful, can, overcome, unleash my abilities, free my creativity and drive, be the best I can be, W.I.N. (what's important now), strive, keep going, go to the end, finish strong" . They're all action words that tell my subconscious brain to get into gear, align on purpose, and generate the power to meet the challenge.

Inspiration is a quality that also touches the emotional side of your being. For example, you might say "I am focused and apply the energy to overcome obstacles". However, if you were to use a formula that contains words that call upon your emotions, the statement would be more empowering, and moving. A reformulation of the statement could be, "I strive to maintain a tight focus and this empowers me to overcome all obstacles that stand in the way of my success".

You may not agree at first, but if you close your eyes, take a few deep breaths, and repeat this statement with feeling, you will notice the difference in a short period of time.

Inspiring words touch your subconscious and cause it to get animated. When everything is said and done, we accomplish what we set out to do only when we have sufficient inspiration to cause powerful movement, felt all the way through our body.

In line with the drive to life mastery, vision is a key element of the work necessary to set a direction. The total effort starts with setting the compass, then establishing a path to where we want to get. Using a detailed and comprehensive description of the desired outcome will strengthen the direction of the compass. To create maximum momentum, you will be well-served to include inspiring words that reach your subconscious brain and create the **PULL** thus making execution effort-less.

AÏM FOR LIFE MASTERY™

In the end, life is much more fun when you don't have to strain so much.

Setting your compass by way of a compelling vision will go a long way to make your life much more interesting.

The Power of Vision in Action

I want to share the story of Ken, one of my clients, to show the power of a compelling vision (names changed to protect identity).

Many years ago, I met Ken through a common acquaintance. He was a struggling business guy who had a dream of becoming a professional coach in the National Football League (NFL). However, his dream seemed to be a world apart from his reality. He had played football and coached at minor levels, but he was a long way from achieving what seemed to be the impossible.

As Rome was not built in a day, Ken first took a few years to straighten out his personal life, moving from a destructive relationship to a loving one based on common goals. He got married and had two kids along the way. From a party goer, he transformed himself into a goal seeker. Being familiar with the need to work hard for what he had achieved, Ken crafted a life vision that put him into the NFL as a coach. With countless details, he laid out a plan that would help him climb the ladder of success.

Consecutively, he worked in ever-increasing levels of responsibility until reaching the position of Head Coach in Canada. Along the way, guided by his vision, he took all the necessary steps and met the key people that supported his dream. As he moved along the path he had laid for himself and his family, he progressively discovered ways and means to make things happen, just as he had envisioned.

AÏM FOR LIFE MASTERY™

Today, he is one step away from realizing his lofty goal, that of reaching the NFL. The journey was tortuous at times and required tremendous focus and determination. There were times when it seemed that he was regressing as opposed to moving forward. But one thing is certain, his faith in the will of the Lord and a deep belief in his capability to overcome obstacles along the way have carried him to where the lights are in view.

He was guided by a compelling vision that PULLED him as time went on. And he is about to reap the rewards of staying focused on his goal. As a performance coach, I have lived the trek with him and I assure you that anything is possible once you set your focus on a compelling vision.

After years of observing the power of a clear vision, I am convinced beyond any doubt that "you'll see it when you believe it!"

AÏM FOR LIFE MASTERY™

Revving UP Your Motivation

The root of the word "emotion" comes from the Latin "motus" – the action of moving. The prefix "e" comes from the Latin "ex" – out of. Emotion thus relates to motion out of. Our emotions cause us to move. When we don't have emotions, we remain stationary, kind of dead in our tracks. Emotions are the fuel that drives our motivation. Understanding the nature of our motivation helps to apply full force to our effort.

It's not only crucial to know where you're going, but it's also very important to know **why** you're going there! Defining your reason to seek your vision becomes the second step in the your quest toward Peak Performance.

Motivation Is From Within

Conventional wisdom says that motivation is sparked by outside stimuli such as things, people and events. Motivation is the result of emotions these outside stimuli bring to our brain. But emotions originate from our thought process. And that's totally within us, not outside of us.

Before we can ever feel anything, we must focus on the event, the person, the thing, the experience, whatever the trigger is. And, if there's no past storage of information, then your brain won't be able to assign a meaning to that stimulus. Consequently, it will be impossible to generate a feeling associated with a particular stimulus.

AÏM FOR LIFE MASTERY™

However, if there is an experience associated with an event that is stored in your subconscious brain (long term memory), you will then be compelled to assess the new situation and assign a meaning (mental representation) to it. From the interpretation you attach to the outside stimulus, you will generate a "feeling" or emotion. Sad or joyful, angry or calm, energized or deflated, whatever the information your brain links to a particular stimulus, you will be moved to feel it.

This is called the Pain-Pleasure Principle.

Your interpretation of the activating stimulus either gives you a signal of pain, which causes you to move away from it, or one of pleasure which causes you to move toward it. Since we are emotional beings, we always attribute an emotionally-linked meaning to what is going on outside of us, and the thoughts that we generate inside our head. Only when a person is dead will that principle stop working! Just think, every moment of your waking life, you are moved and motivated by how you feel about something. Awareness of this principle and lessons learned from this process can help you be more focused in applying the peak performance principle, **the right stuff, in the right amount, at the right time™**.

For example, think of the TV images of the earthquake and tsunami in Japan in March 2011 which may have motivated you to action.

It was impossible to remain indifferent watching all the cars, houses and boats being tossed around. We even saw people running for their lives ahead of the wave front. It was heart wrenching, even at thousands of miles distance, to experience the horror those people must have felt. Deep inside, there was an immediate feeling of compassion, and the thoughts arose, "Are we ever lucky to be safe from such disasters. Thank God we live here. I wouldn't want to be caught there, I don't know what I'd do", and right after, "How can I help those people? What can I do to reduce the pain?" We were moved to action, thinking about those poor people, and moved to give money to the relief fund.

Motivation is always at work. Whether the feeling or emotion is good or bad, there will always be an action in line with it. It might not always be what you'd like, but there will be a reaction. It's how we're made.

If the natural reaction is to generate a feeling (or emotion) once we have interpreted the stimulus, why not learn to use the principle (or mechanism) really well, and use it to our advantage?

Why not develop an awareness of how you react to situations, define the emotion derived from the event or stimulus, and learn how you tend to react in the moment? Maybe this can serve as a basis to identify what to change in your way of thinking, or how you view things so that ultimately, you are able to guide your emotional response? Just a thought.

Almost every day of our life, we hear something that doesn't fit with our beliefs and values. "They have it all wrong!" you'll hear yourself say. And then, the rant and rave goes on for a couple of minutes about how the world is going nuts. Much emotional and mental energy is spent formulating how wrong their thinking is, and how this attitude or point of view will lead us all to doom! In the end, all that saliva and spouted words are useless. They won't make a hoot of difference, except to annoy those around you, or worse still, give a stranger the impression that you're emotionally off your rocker!

The words you heard weren't what motivated your rant. Rather, it was your deep beliefs or values that interpreted the statements as being "wrong". The motivation was not from outside, but well within you.

I'd like to reassure you that, try as you may, you'll never totally eliminate emotional upset from your life!

AÏM FOR LIFE MASTERY™

I'm not saying you should become a robot. After all, you're a human being, and emotions are natural. What I'm saying is that you can raise your own performance by recognizing that your feelings (emotions) are your own, and no one can affect them if you won't let them. You can decide how you feel. You can decide how you react. You can decide to choose "life mastery"!

Your Reasons Are Your Reasons

I know what you're probably thinking right now. It's quite a challenge to accept that whatever feeling you harbor is the result of your own thinking, and nothing else. Of course, this flies in the face of our natural tendency to point the finger and say, "he made me do it". However, any way you look at it, we are ultimately responsible for how we feel!

But enough of that. Let's move forward to what we can do about how we feel. Often, people will question your right to a certain feeling. You'll hear, "you have no right to feel that way". Or often, someone will question why you feel a certain way. In their opinion, it's obvious that they have no idea what caused you to generate the feeling you've expressed.

The fact is that "your reasons are your reasons".

Let's open the lid on that statement. We all come from a different place: we have different life experiences, different education, different exposure, different cultural background, and different interests. It's said that, "We have only one thing in common, and that is… we are all different." The drama arises from the fact that we too often forget this reality with respect to the people around us.

Instead of realizing that we all have a different perspective, we have a tendency to judge as "wrong" another person's point of view. We do this because we view things through our own filters, and not theirs. Inevitably, that creates friction if not discord, and the result is the non-acceptance of another person's feelings or reaction. We recoil, analyze, judge, and assign the label "wrong". This leads us to reject the other person on the basis of **feeling** (or motivation).

However, your reasons are your reasons. And until someone provides information or facts that help assign a different interpretation to the stimulus, you have a right to your feelings, and your motivation is fully valid.

Without dwelling on the fact that your reasons are your reasons, there will be times when you're unsure of your reasons, and you'll back off. However, in the long run, you will feel resentment -

> "Resentment is like taking poison and then waiting for the other person to die."
> Malachy McCourt

resentment for the other person or resentment toward yourself.

Your self-esteem will be affected, and you will lose the edge to be a peak performer. You will continue to be burdened by the perception that you don't have the right to your feelings. By itself, it will be your choice. In the big picture, however, you will continue to undermine the fuel that makes you charge ahead. The uncertainty that was subconsciously created will act as a barrier to the full use of your maximum potential.

In conclusion, getting your motivation up for an effort is totally under your influence. One thing you should always remember is that if you wait for something, or someone to ignite your motivation, you'll wait a long time! You have the power to motivate yourself. Awareness is the key. And the sooner you decide to dig deep inside and recognize your reasons to be motivated, the sooner the power of internal motivation will grow and become second nature. You'll gain the ability to fuel up your motivation.

AÏM FOR LIFE MASTERY™

Good Days and Bad Days (all the same)

How often have you heard this? "I'm having a bad day", or "This is a good day".

To peak performers, they're all "days"! And you owe it to yourself to make them work for you. Otherwise, your motivation will be affected, and your drive may suffer at the worst times.

You see, whatever you're doing on any given day, good or bad, you have the responsibility to make the best of it. Of course, if you don't believe that everything that happens to you is the result of your action or inaction, you'll point the finger at external reasons or factors to explain your undesired outcomes.

Since we all have the freedom to choose, I grant you that you're free to call it a bad day or a good day. In the end, as I have made a choice to focus on peak performance and life mastery, I must caution you that your choice of good or bad can interfere with your mastery of Peak Performance!

Bottom line – it's about fuelling your motivation.

Programming yourself to assign "bad" to your day will defeat the momentum that your compass's direction has created. "Bad" will act as an anchor that slows down your journey to success. If you don't believe me, make a conscious effort to qualify your day as good or bad, then take note of its impact on your feelings. You'll soon notice the difference!

If you want to maximize results and minimize effort, you'll act in a way that liberates your full potential.

Planting Guardrails

It's necessary to know where you want to go, and the reasons why you want to go there.

However, we must recognize that there is no perfect situation. And too often, there will be distractions or unexpected events that will cloud the view of the vision, and weaken the reasons for working to get there. That's when the guardrails – a set of sound values – will ensure that you stay the course, that you remain focused on the end play, that you keep on trying despite reversals in your progress.

In order to render the journey durable and strengthen your resolve so that there is no regret, you'll want to sit back and review what you value in life. Research shows that if you have a well-defined set of five or six values in your awareness pack as you travel, you'll never falter very far from the course you've set.

Therefore, once a direction (vision) and reason (motivation) are clearly set and defined, it's time to select the values (guardrails) that will keep you on the road to your vision.

Values Are for Life

Over the course of your life, you've gained a set of values that keep you on the road of life, and prevent you, most of the time, from slipping into the "ditch" on your earthly journey. I suspect that you have an idea of what "ditch" means. But just to make sure we're on the same page, let me explain.

AÏM FOR LIFE MASTERY™

Values are like guardrails on a risky road, with deep ditches or sudden drops along the way.

On highways, those dangerous places are usually protected by guardrails, a fence-type equipment that helps a car out of control stay on the road and prevent a major accident.

The same applies for the road of life.

Once in a while, we're off our game. We forget what we're all about. We inadvertently sacrifice blood, sweat, and tears for the sake of a fleeting moment. We lose control of the wheel (life guidance), and start weaving to the point where we hit the edge of our desired journey. We let costly curves take us away from the straight line to the goal. We wander wildly away from the right direction. We end up wasting time and energy.

That's when values come into play and act as guardrails. They're the "out of the blue" reminder that going along with friends on a certain trek (whatever) is not in line with our intended path. Or we might be tempted to steal something but soon come to our senses, and think of the consequences. Spending foolishly on an item or activity that doesn't help us reach desired outcomes can also be a major obstacle on the road to Peak Performance.

Values are those things or actions that we've established as MUST DOs in order to be aligned to our purpose.

For example, you may value <u>respect</u>.

That value will cause you to take notice and refuse to act, if you're faced with a decision that will show "disrespect".

Or you may value <u>honesty</u>.

That value will make you feel bad if you're dishonest in a certain situation.

AÏM FOR LIFE MASTERY™

Another value might be <u>communication</u>. The act of communicating is of great value in any situation involving people working toward a common goal.

This value will guide you to make an effort to communicate purposefully in order to produce the results you want.

Values act as boundaries to guide our daily efforts. They're at work 100% of the time. They provide the caution flags that help us stay true to ourselves.

I'm sure you can already imagine that there are a lot more than five or six values that support your life as you want it to be. Research has identified no less than 147 values (see Appendix 2 for a list of values identified in research). It's important to share your values with the people around you. That's where selecting five or six main values enables you to verbalize more easily where you stand, and explain your position when faced with a certain situation.

You will do well to take time to reflect, consider and identify those values that will keep you on the road to your destiny

A differentiation can be helpful here to separate your beliefs from your values.

We talked earlier about the fuel – motivation. Motivation is based on our <u>beliefs</u>.

Remember Gandhi's words; beliefs become my destiny. What we believe causes us to get up in the morning, to take action, to drive with determination toward the desired goal.

What we value acts as reminders of HOW to journey to the goal. Values are for life. They bring certainty to our drive. They provide the compass to our life. They're important in moments of forgetfulness.

AÏM FOR LIFE MASTERY™

By this time, you're probably wondering what this has to do with Peak Performance. When you're overtaken by the emotion of the moment, values will act as guardrails to keep you on your road to personal success.

Identifying your values, knowing what they are, casting them in the framework of peak performance, and re-visiting them once in a while, will ensure that they become like guardians of your life.

Once you're clear on the values that will guide your effort in all circumstances, you will automatically increase your performance.

Knowing the Boundaries

Knowing the boundaries means being aware of what you want out of life.

This brings to mind the need for hard work in identifying who you are, and what you want for a complete life, one where you'll feel that you've achieved everything you set out to achieve. If your values are the guardrails for your journey, those values won't have as much meaning if you have not defined the boundaries of your life.

By boundaries, I mean the limits of everything you can be and want to achieve in your lifetime. For example, a person who has a life goal of building a family should look closely at how many children he or she wants to have, and what kind of education they will get. That will help to define the person who will be the lifemate in this journey, and the resources that will be needed along the way to pay for the education.

One way to define your boundaries might be to define what you've already accomplished in your life!

It's a positive approach, one that often helps to clarify your view of what you want.

AÏM FOR LIFE MASTERY™

Here's an exercise that will help you define your boundaries (Appendix 10 – Life Successes Inventory). Take a piece of paper (8.5 x 11) and divide it in three sections. On the left side, list all the achievements in your life where you felt that you performed in a way that produced the best results. Don't think of these in sequence. Just brainstorm and write ideas as they come to mind. Write until you can't think of anything else that is memorable by its positive result.

In the other two columns, for each of the events or situations noted, list how you felt and what you learned from the way you acted. Be honest and positive. Recognize the benefit to self and to others. Be proud of the achievement, but stay humble just the same. You'll discover in your reflection that there are moments in your life where you didn't recognize what was going on. You took everything for granted. You didn't realize that you had acted in line with beliefs and values that establish the boundaries of the path guiding you through the event.

This happened to me when I realized that my marriage had ended back in 1986. I was lost, wondering why I should continue to live. After all, the life I had committed to was no more. In my search for an answer, I travelled to Switzerland. There, perched on a ledge, halfway up the famous Matterhorn, I decided I had a very good reason to live. You see, up to that moment, I had serious thoughts of ending it all. Even sitting there, I thought how easy it would be to let myself fall down a crevasse, and disappear forever. But I remembered that I had three children who needed me. I started doing an inventory of what I had to offer. The rest is history. This book is a tangible sign of my discovery.

You might not be this close to despair, but the exercise I have suggested will definitely help in knowing your boundaries. As with anything else, doing it once will bring some things to the surface.

AÏM FOR LIFE MASTERY™

Repeating the exercise and reviewing your results will deepen your understanding of who you are, and help define your boundaries, and the values that keep you on the road. Do yourself a favour and take time right now to fill out your sheet. You might be surprised to find that you need more than one sheet! It will be well worth your time to discover your boundaries!

Be True To Yourself

Values are your guardrails to stay the course, to keep your eye on the road, to guide your efforts in line with your life vision. Keep them in mind as you take responsibility to make sure that you remain true to yourself. Peak performance depends on the right stuff, in the right amount, at the right time, and that can only happen when you are solidly in full awareness of your values.

Your values will help to ensure that you stay true to yourself. However, you will also want to remain alert and flexible so that you avoid putting yourself into a straight jacket when conditions demand a shift in approach.

As we human beings have a habit of developing tunnel vision, you will want to remain vigilant and be conscious of your values and boundaries at all times. That consciousness will help minimize the effort you apply to stay on course in a changing environment.

Remaining aware of your guardrails will also enable you to be true to yourself in most situations, in a somewhat automatic way. Your increased consciousness will help reduce the moments when you have to regret an unwanted behaviour. And you can be sure that such moments will happen again. After all, you're not a machine.

AÏM FOR LIFE MASTERY™

Beware Incongruence

A word about incongruence. In this case, the feeling of discomfort, of uneasiness without cause, of disappointment with self, will arise if you're not totally true to yourself.

There's a built-in feature in our subconscious brain, a mental model that acts as a constant monitor of our actions.

When we violate our values, and we're not true to ourselves, we develop a feeling of discomfort – incongruence, misalignment with our values.

Listen for that signal at all times. It will be a sure indicator that you're not true to yourself, or that you're infringing upon your values. When that happens, reflect on the situation or event. You will most likely recognize the disconnect between what you value in life, and the action you took in the moment.

Be true to yourself in those circumstances, and take action to rectify the behaviour that brought about the discomfort. In the end, you'll live with less stress. Living with incongruence is a slow, winding road to stress. It's the gnawing feeling that something is not right. It's an ever-present feeling that you could have been better or done things differently in a certain situation. It usually develops into a feeling of regret that makes you say, "If only I'd …."

Staying focused on your vision, and maintaining clarity about the reasons why you want to realize your dream will usually work to drive you to the result you seek. However, the journey will never be without bumps and curves on the road. Since you want to be a peak performer who maximizes results and minimizes effort, you will do well to keep your values in mind.

Values are the guardrails that help keep a vehicle on the road through dangerous stretches. Values will act on automatic to

AÏM FOR LIFE MASTERY™

bring you back on course when you lose your direction because of unexpected distractions. Values will help you avoid major accidents in your life when you're weakened by the burden of your life events.

Remember to review and if needed, recast your values at the same time as you review your vision (where you are going?) and the reasons (why?) for your existence. Like anything else, practice makes perfect. If you continually remind yourself of your values (live with integrity), you'll build a solid set of guardrails that will help you stay on course no matter the severity of the circumstances because you will have programmed the path of the peak performer in your life!

Key Points to Remember

* The whole process of establishing peak performance is underpinned by **AïM**, the recipe to raise awareness of your required or innate ability, internalize it, integrate it into your routine, and practice it often to develop mastery of the ability.

* In order to be good at one thing, you must understand the concept you are applying. In this book, Peak Performance is defined as **the right stuff, in the right amount, at the right time™**. Keep focused on the appropriate action under a given circumstance, making sure you use the correct amount (enough but not too much), at the right time so that you produce the optimum result you are seeking.

* Focus is the key element to generate drive and move in the right direction. The cornerstone of an effective focus is to have a detailed and comprehensive image (vision) of where you want to go. When the vision is clear, the PULL is strong and reaching the desired goal is much easier.

AÏM FOR LIFE MASTERY™

*   Motivation is from within. Don't look outside for someone to kick start you. Be clear on the reasons that get you going every day. Remind yourself that only you can pump up your motivation. Focus on positive words to drive you to action.

*   Your values are guardrails that will keep you on track on your journey to peak performance. Be sure to know what they are and use them when in doubt.

AÏM FOR LIFE MASTERY™

PART III – PROGRAMMING PEAK PERFORMANCE

STAYING ON TRACK...

PART I   Setting Up The Journey

PART II   Building The Foundation

PART III   Programming Peak Performance

PART IV   Releasing Your Brakes

APPENDICES

AÏM FOR LIFE MASTERY™

We're now getting into the serious work of transformation at which this book is aiming. Let's list the six steps that will compose the journey you will undertake to create new thinking pathways (programs) that will make you a peak performer.

Step 1 – Quieting the brain: setting up to receive the commands

Step 2 – Reframing Self-talk: learning the affirmation technique

Step 3 – Seeing the future today: learning the visualization technique

Step 4 – Expressing Gratitude: installing a positive lens

Step 5 – Creating mastery: designing repetition for the automatic

Step 6 – Anchoring Peak Performance: implementing a trigger for quick access

Each of these steps is described to provide insight on how to plan and execute your approach toward peak performance. Keep the process in mind, and I guarantee you'll be a peak performer.

Step One – Quieting the Brain

In all studies done on the capability of the brain, one aspect is beyond any doubt - we can all handle a multitude of stimuli at once. It is indeed a wonder of our species. Just like a computer, our brain runs at super speeds and jumps around thoughts in fractions of a second. Research shows that we usually manage or produce over 50,000 thoughts per day, waking time. If we assume that we're awake about sixteen hours a day on average, then that would mean that we have roughly one thought every two seconds. Incredible isn't it!!

This means that our capacity to think is awesome. But when it comes to focus, just the opposite is true. Hold that thought! Since we habitually manage many thoughts at once, we do it more or less effectively. The problem is, when we want to slow down that process, it becomes very difficult, if not nearly impossible.

> "This art of resting the mind and the power of dismissing from it all care and worry is probably one of the secrets of energy in our great men."
> — **Captain J. A. Hadfield,** Author

So, in order to become effective in creating peak performance, it's necessary to learn how to quiet our brain. Somehow, we want to slow down the rapid cycling, and induce ourselves into a more moderate mode, so that our concentration becomes easier to maintain.

Quieting our brain is absolutely fundamental in peak performance. The best technique I've encountered is the one by Herbert Benson[7], the father of the relaxation response. His understanding of the mind-body connection has led to the design of a method to affect the brain by the body position.

Maxwell Maltz[8] also expounded on the benefits of relaxation in his theory on developing and changing self-image. Through his work with plastic surgery patients, he identified the need to free up the brain of unwanted concerns and negative emotions before any work to create new thinking pathways can be done. As he puts it, relaxation is like going into "an emotional decompression chamber". To be able to refocus and realign, a person must remove the cloud of emotions that blur the picture of the desired state. Relaxation progressively frees our mind to think clearly.

---

[7] Benson, Herbert. *The Relaxation Response.* Harper. First edition. 1976
[8] Maltz, Maxwell. *Psycho-Cybernetics: A New Way to Get More Living Out of Life.* Prentice Hall. Ney York 1960

AÏM FOR LIFE MASTERY™

Milton Erickson[9] was a psychiatrist and researcher who was renowned for his hypnosis and family therapy. Among his findings were concepts related to non verbal communication and the power of the unconscious mind – both as a result of having had polio at age 17. For a long time, he was unable to speak. He managed to recover his speech through mental exercises. His personal experience further supports the mind-body connection concept advanced by Herbert Benson whose research showed that anything expressed by the body was reflected in the brain, and any thought in the brain was reflected in how the body feels.

A student of Erickson, Ernest Lawrence Rossi[10], produced a treatise on ways and means to use rhythms effectively. Our body is regulated by rhythms. The one Rossi focused on was the **Ultradian Rhythm**. This natural 90-120 minute interval produces a peak and valley movement in our activation. At the peak, we're more alert and able to produce. In the valley, we tend to be more relaxed. However, modern society has pushed us to override this natural rhythm cheating us of the beneficial valley moment where our physiology tends to re-balance. We've learned to stay at, or near the peak all day, thereby accumulating stress hormones. So we get tired as the day wears on. Learning to create the valley mode during relaxation allows us to rest, relax, and recharge. That knowledge was added to the building of the process for quieting the brain that I'm proposing.

Application of Yoga principles have also contributed to the integration of breathing into the process. For instance, opening the palms of your hands to the sky acts as a magnet to surrounding energy. Breathing in through the nose and holding your breath allows further expansion of your inner self, making room for relaxation.

---

[9] Erickson, Milton. Read about him in Wikipedia; enter Milton H. Erickson
[10] Rossi, Ernest Lawrence. *The 20 Minute Break.: Using the New Science of Ultradian Rhythms.* Jeremy P. Tarcher. 1991

AÏM FOR LIFE MASTERY™

Further, the work of Bandler and Grinder[11] in Neuro Linguistic Programming has supplied clarification on some of the benefits to be sought in applying a relaxation technique.

Finally, based in part on all the works cited above, I've developed a technique that has been proven beyond doubt that we can affect the activity of our brain in a way that allows us to rewire our brain or create new thinking pathways more easily than previously thought. I've witnessed it in my own practice, both as a user of the process and a coach.

A short write up of this technique referred to as the **3R Process**© is included in Appendix 3. It explains the process and provides a calendar to assist in the implementation of the technique to learn how to breathe to create a calm state.

It was a widely held belief that once you had developed a certain habit, it could not be changed easily. How often have we heard: "It's just the way I am", as an excuse to behave in a certain way. Conventional wisdom said that it was difficult, and even nearly impossible to change a habit. In more recent decades, research has proven otherwise.

Techniques can be used to reprogram our brain, and the transformation can be made permanent, just as we believed all along. The key is to have the **motivation to do what is necessary** to implant the new thinking pathway, essentially making the effort to change the way we think.

When looking to quiet your brain, remember that it starts inside the subconscious.

When you learn to quiet the subconscious brain, it becomes possible to gain mastery of your thinking process. Once mastery

---

[11] Bandler, Richard and Grinder, John. Co-founders of the research that produced the understanding of Neuro Linguistic Programming. Authors of *Frogs to Princes* and many other books on the subject.

of your thinking process is reached, then you can direct your thinking more easily and produce the results you desire, mentally, emotionally, and psychologically. In order to provide a structured and systematic approach to relaxation and quieting your brain, the following breaks down the various parts of the technique for better understanding and application.

Posture for Quiet

Based on the principle of the mind-body connection, it's possible to affect what goes on inside your brain through our physical posture. Let me clarify. Earl Nightingale, a pioneer in the field of personal development had these reflections on the concept:

- Your body moves in the direction of your predominant thoughts.
- Your mind harbours what your body manifests.

If we apply this concept, it follows that the posture adopted by your body will affect what you think. Why not try this out to prove it? Stand up and roll your shoulders forward. Drop your head down, chin on your chest. Stay in the position for at least two minutes. Now, keeping that stance, check what's happening in your mind. Can you think a positive thought? Can you think a joyful thought? Can you feel energetic? My guess is that it will be difficult, if not impossible.

When rolling your shoulders forward and dropping your head down, you've pinched your breathing passage. Air finds its way in with more difficulty. A shortage of oxygen reduces brain capacity. Not only that - a number of body functions are slowed down by the posture, thus reducing the flow of energy throughout. Your capability to think clearly is reduced.

AÏM FOR LIFE MASTERY™

Now reverse the position. Stand tall, shoulders back, head up looking straight ahead, and breathe normally. Count to 120, then check how you feel. Can you think dark thoughts? Negative thoughts? Low energy thoughts? More than likely, you're now unable to easily think negatively. You're naturally energized. You're breathing more freely, and your body functions are freed to work as they should.

Now that you've experienced the link, can you see the possibility of affecting your thoughts by the way you position yourself? Do you think it's possible to affect your thinking by the way you behave or control your movements? I hope you do, because learning about linking your posture to your state of mind is one of the key elements in creating new thinking pathways!

In the case of quieting your subconscious brain, it follows that if you adopt a quiet position, you will induce quiet in your brain – makes sense, doesn't it?

In the **3R Process**©, I recommend a sitting position. The main reason for sitting is that I want to teach you how to create quiet brain activity in any awakened situation, no matter what activity is going on. You can use this method at will, in tight situations. After all, you wouldn't want to have to lie down to relax yourself in the middle of a meeting or while at the job!

To ensure that your whole body is invested in this process, I recommend that you sit on a straight chair, not a sofa (that's too comfortable) so that you stay alert. You should choose a quiet place, to minimize distractions. Turning the lights down is also conducive to quieting the brain. Take your shoes off, and place your feet flat on the floor. Comfortably lay your hands on your thighs, palms up to absorb the surrounding energy (or at least aiming up if uncomfortable in the flat position). Hold your shoulders back and head up to free up your breathing passage.

AÏM FOR LIFE MASTERY™

Allowing the air in and out freely is fundamental to build oxygen levels.

Of course, if you want to facilitate going to sleep, you can use the lying position before going to sleep, increasing your body's ability to rejuvenate.

Breathe for Quiet

If posture is key in initiating brain quietness, a breathing method is also a key element to help quiet brain activity. This is extracted from Yoga principles, and aims to help your body create harmony between brain activity and breathing. The breathing program is outlined in the instructions below.

The concept is based on breathing IN through the nose, HOLDing your breath for a few seconds, then breathing OUT through your mouth. The air through the nose massages the nasal membranes and contributes to the soothing effect on the brain. Holding your breath follows a yoga concept that allows expansion of body molecules to create flexibility. Breathing OUT through the mouth aims at creating a restriction with your lips so that the diaphragm works gently to push the air out.

Breathing from the diaphragm means that if you put your hand on your upper chest, there shouldn't be any movement. The movement should be totally from the tummy, allowing the full use of your lungs to exchange oxygen and release carbon dioxide. Bringing in maximum air brings in maximum oxygen, and maximum oxygen means maximum availability for body functions – better performance, and elimination of fatigue!

Breathing in this way also produces a massaging effect on your internal organs, causing them to reject toxins and other products of body functions, thus creating a recharging effect.

AÏM FOR LIFE MASTERY™

This activity is the foundation of my **Rest / Relax / Recharge**© concept to produce relaxation at will.

Focus for Quiet

In sports, we often hear this expression; "Focus! Focus! you need to focus!". Most of the time, those doing the reminding and those being reminded don't really know what this means. It's said by rote, until redundant, without really producing anything but further tension and anxiety in the person who is performing.

If the goal is to quiet brain activity, then we should use a mental activity while sitting and breathing that will be conducive to quieting the brain. There are a number of ways to do this. Here are three that have proven to be effective in slowing down the constant subconscious flow of thoughts going on in our brain, and narrowing our focus:

Focus on one air molecule
While breathing in and out, imagine that the air you breathe is composed of millions of specs, all shiny and bright, like golden specs floating in the air. Pick one up in your line of sight, and imagine it entering your nose, travelling down your air pipe to your lungs, exchanging with the blood, and coming back up the airway, through your mouth, and out in front of you. Imagine that the golden shiny spec comes out greyish and dull, no shine to it. It's the image of the cleansing process that's going on in your body, at the oxygen exchange level. You're sending a message of benefit to your subconscious brain. This is good!

Create a STOP sign
While you breathe, close your eyes and imagine seeing a STOP sign. As you breathe IN, HOLD, and OUT, check your brain activity. If your thoughts start racing, call up the STOP sign, see it, and say STOP!

AÏM FOR LIFE MASTERY™

Imagine the Process
Focus on your breathing. Picture the inhaling first step as a ramp up (like the expansion of your chest as you breathe IN). During the HOLD step, picture a horizontal line, moving from left to right. When you start breathing OUT, picture a ramp down back to the level you started at in the breathing cycle. At the end of the OUT step, travel from the end of that ramp back to the start of the up ramp. Continue this visual exercise as you go through the IN-HOLD-OUT cycle.

Expected Result
The final outcome is that you link all of your posture, your breathing, and your mind state in a quiet place where you learn to slow down the brain activity. There are a few reasons to remain still and mindful during your relaxation exercise:

- One is that the quieting impact on your subconscious brain is increased. Therefore, the quieting transformation will happen faster.

- A second concept at work is that by teaching your brain to slow down, you're inducing your subconscious brain to move to the alpha brainwave state (8-14 cycles per second) where it becomes more easily programmed. See Appendix 4 for a short explanation of the various brain activity levels.

- A third impact is that while doing the exercise, your body and mind are linked in a parallel state of calm. Based on the mind-body connection, 20-30 days of focused practice, morning and night, will teach your body to respond to a quiet brain, and conversely, your brain will be programmed to go quiet when you take the **3R Posture**©.

Ultimately, this exercise is the first building block in the creation of new thinking pathways.

AÏM FOR LIFE MASTERY™

By quieting your brain, you make it more suggestible, ready to accept new thoughts as suggestions for transformation. It essentially becomes a non-destructive transformation of brain synapses, dendrites and neurons to store and send new information (neurotransmitters) by which your subconscious brain will be able to produce new results on command. In the next chapter, we will review the second step to reprogramming your brain – affirmations commonly called the little voice or self-talk.

AÏM FOR LIFE MASTERY™

Step Two – Reframing Self-talk

Just as we want to slow down or quiet down our brain to reach a peak performance mode, we need to gain more mastery of the little voice, that devilish yapper that has a tendency to torpedo, or at least, distract our conscious brain from its task.

Here, it's necessary to review the concept of programming.

Quieting the brain is an exercise to prepare our subconscious brain to receive new information in a way that will be productive, effective, lasting, and will bring about a change in mental capability.

Our brain can store information that it can use constantly, effectively, to re-create a desired behaviour at will. The proof is that we've done this since we were infants. How do you think you learned to ride a bicycle?

We store information constantly, and our long-term memory ensures that this information is available when required. The problem is, we don't consciously know where that information is stored, and therefore, we have trouble at times remembering how to use it. You might remember how to ride the bicycle, but you don't always remember how to deal effectively with the bully across the street.

The problem is that our subconscious brain knows where the information is stored but retrieves it randomly and not necessarily in the way that is most productive.

An example would be our disdain for a certain food. We have no idea why we learned to dislike it, but we don't like it. Most likely, the information was stored many years ago, and the smell or taste is lodged where the autonomous system is. Sometimes, just tasting the food rekindles our original liking, erasing the bad memory. That's just the way our brain works.

The beauty of that capability is that it can be used to our advantage. We can wilfully choose to reprogram our subconscious brain using the same principles. In this case, we're talking about using the lack of capacity of the subconscious brain to know the difference between what is imagined and what is real. In essence, we can fool our subconscious brain to accept an idea as fact, and it will not resist it. Only our conscious brain can assess, evaluate, and reject an idea. Your subconscious brain is like a sponge. It just absorbs what is offered as long as the thought or stimulus doesn't contravene your beliefs or values.

The five senses are the passageways to the subconscious brain, like a keyboard to a computer. Whatever we sense visually, through our hearing, through smell, taste or touch gets recorded. Based on this, we can decide what we will feed to our subconscious brain, and install the programs we want to use. In this instance, touch, taste, and smell are not the easiest to work with.

It's therefore left to the visual and auditory channels to absorb the information we want to program. The other senses can be used to anchor more solidly the idea by association with a taste, a smell, or a touch.

The Constant Chatter

To achieve Peak Performance, it's super important to stop and reflect on one of the most unconscious processes that go on inside our head.

> Can you imagine 50,000 thoughts racing through your mind in a waking day?
> Can you hear the constant chatter?

Research has shown that we have over 50,000 thoughts per day running through our mind. Many of those thoughts initiate a reflective process in our neo-cortex, the thinking part of the brain. And since we have a tendency to verbalize our thoughts (that's how we formulate ideas), we carry on a self-conversation almost continually.

You have no doubt heard or read about the "little voice", the self-talk that we entertain within ourselves.

It's ongoing and explores connections in our thinking, sorts out options, and likely enables our decision process, not to mention other thinking processes such as evaluating what we see, assigning a meaning to words we hear, gauging the level of our preference when we taste something.

The little voice is almost always in action. It's a useful tool that helps us make sense of our surroundings, and of the stimuli that bombard us constantly through the five senses.

If we vulgarize the process, it can be described as the constant chatter that's going on in our head. That chatter comes from our thinking process. Our thinking process is more or less automatic as it reacts to the environment captured through our senses, and is the product of our beliefs and values applied to our judging system.

> "The loudest and most influential voice you hear is your own inner voice, your self-critic. It can work for you or against you, depending on the messages you allow."
> — **Keith Harrell,** Dr. Attitude

Often, this chatter is a big help to see things more clearly. However, at other times, it can be the source of confusion and misconception, since the chatter usually acts on stored information that may be faulty. But since it is part of our thinking process, and we know that we can affect the thinking process;

---

then it follows that we can also influence the constant chatter, and influence what it will say.

Consequently, we can influence and modify the little voice, and in the end, make it a pathway rather than a barrier to performance.

The Power of Words

The little voice or self-talk is based on the use of words. However, there are times when words can only express thoughts with great difficulty. Perhaps it's a reflection of the disconnect with the process of imagery that our brain uses to interpret the stimuli bombarding us. As human beings, we rely on words to express our thoughts, to communicate. Unfortunately, words are often too weak to express what we're thinking. Nonetheless, we use words because they're the only means of making sense of the thoughts that run through our mind.

In a communication filled with emotions, some research has proposed that words contain only about seven percent of the essence of the message. Voice (tone, speed, pitch, inflection, etc.) account for 38 percent, and a full 55 percent is contained in body language and how we appear[12].

> In face-to-face business communication, research has shown that the message is composed of three main aspects in the following percentages:
> Words – 7 %
> Voice – 38 %
> Gestures – 55 %
> It makes sense to listen with your eyes!

But when we consider communication within ourselves, words take on an all too different character. When formulated, they

---

[12] Mehrabian, Albert and Wiener, Morton (1967). "Decoding of Inconsistent Communications". Journal of Personality and Social Psychology 6 (1): 109–114

resonate inside our head and take on an entirely different significance, the impact of which is hardly recognized.

Take the example of a person who curses.

A curse is an expression of anger, frustration, hurt, anxiety, excitement, enthusiasm, or whatever emotion that spills over the boundaries of normal. The use of the curse word reinforces the feeling inside. And for the one who utters it, it deepens the feeling or emotion. It anchors the emotion more deeply in the subconscious.

Since we are creatures of habit, a curse entertained is a curse uttered. People who curse have developed the habit of cursing, just as people who don't curse have an ingrained habit of not cursing. There's a reason why we develop verbal habits – repetition, repetition, repetition.

Now, is the little voice or self-talk or internal chatter not a habit developed over time?

Words harden through repetition, and they anchor our way of seeing and expressing ourselves. The little voice becomes a habit that's hard to break if it weakens us. On the flip side, it can be a powerful force in dealing with a number of challenging situations. It's an automatic response to a stimulus, and the habit saves a lot of time. Sounds like a process that could be used to your advantage if you chose to use it, doesn't it?

Take for example the ongoing chatter of two persons; one is successful in business, the other fails at every venture he attempts. If we could listen to their respective self-talk, I'm sure that the successful person would sound like, "Here's another opportunity; let's see how I can make good at it." Is this not the way you face a new challenge when you believe you can succeed? On the flip side, the little voice of the failing person would likely be, "I don't know about this; I've had other

opportunities and there are always things that cause me to fail."
The tone is diametrically opposed. One thinks he can succeed.
The other looks for reasons to weaken his capacity to succeed.
And it all happens on automatic. As Denis Waitley[13] says,
"Winning is a habit, and so is losing."

No Aim, No Hit

Here is a statement of the obvious.

If you've ever shot a gun in a target practice, or a bow and arrow,
or just thrown a ball or object at something, you soon found out
that a random throw or aim leads to a random result.

If you don't aim, you might
hit, but the potential for a
high number of hits is low.
That principle applies in

> If you don't aim, you might hit, but the potential for a high number of hits is LOW.

every aspect of life. We must aim if we're to be successful in
hitting the target.

Now, you may think that if you're only practicing the actual action
of throwing, or shooting, it doesn't really matter, does it? All that
matters is learning the feel of the action, so that you develop
muscle memory. With time, the repetition of the action becomes
much easier, and the ability to use the action or tool grows. You
become skilled at it.

Ability doesn't mean efficiency.

You can practice all you want shooting a bow and arrow, if you
don't have the Bull's-eye in front of you, you'll be shooting at
nothing. You need a target to produce performance.

The same applies to peak performance. You can wish to obtain
certain results through focused action, but if there isn't an

---

[13] Waitley, Denis. *The Psychology of Winning.* Audio-cassette program. Nightingale-Conant. 1990

accurate aim, your rate of success will be left to chance. In the case of using the little voice or self-talk effectively and efficiently, the same principle must be applied. To get the anticipated result, you must choose to aim. You had better choose the right, correct, and accurate words. Otherwise, your efforts will lead exactly to where you're aiming – NOWHERE.

If we are to change self-talk to make it useful, then we must reframe it to produce the desired result. An example of reframing might be as follows: instead of using a negative formula to stop a bad eating habit (I don't want to be fat), it might be more useful and powerful to use "I am at my ideal weight".

Aim the statement to say what you mean, and provide your subconscious brain a clear direction of what you want. Aim and you will hit. The concept is universal. And the outcome is guaranteed.

Powerful Words, Powerful Results

If we address the issue of self-talk, it's not only necessary to aim to hit, but it's also necessary to emphasize and strengthen the message.

You may wish to gain confidence in a certain situation, but it will take longer if you only nudge your subconscious brain instead of giving it a firm command. Just like a horse, the subconscious brain is hard-headed and requires a strong push to be touched by our words. If you

> I figured that if I said it enough, I would convince the world that I was really the greatest.
> - **Muhammad Ali**

want quick results, powerful words are needed to create powerful results. Many famous people have shown us the validity of this principle. For example, Muhammad Ali was the greatest, but his self-talk certainly had a big part in taking him from obscurity to being the most remarkable boxer who ever lived.

Powerful refers not only to the *type* of word. It also refers to *how you will use* the words. If you simply repeat them in a monotonous, unfeeling manner, there will hardly be an impact on your subconscious brain. Remember the subconscious brain (the horse) is very strong! To increase the impact of your affirmations, you must link them to feelings so that you are not only hearing them, but you are associating <u>emotions</u> to them. Now your brain and whole being start to vibrate under the influence of the statements.

For example, if you say "I'm good at what I do", this is pretty simple, emotionless, somewhat neutral, not very specific, and not reaching very deep inside.

If you want to put some punch into the affirmation, how about saying "I believe in my ability to face this challenge; I trust myself and the experience of the past to power me through this event and come out a winner!" That's Peak Performance!

Notice the reference to a solid base, feelings of trust, powerful action verbs and words (believe, face the challenge, power me, winner) that convey a "Can do" attitude to the subconscious brain. The key to powerful mental programming is "…details, details, details…"

In the mental realm, there's a direct relationship between what we get (results), and what we set (mental preparation). Imagine a great result, and you're likely to get it. Imagine a poor result, and you're likely to get it. Many times we don't realize how much we impact our outcomes by how we think and talk to ourselves. Make sure you use powerful words to enable you to create powerful results!

AÏM FOR LIFE MASTERY™

Let me pause here and give you a concrete example. Many years ago, when I started to coach in peak performance, I led a workshop on controlling negative emotions. Part of the presentation addressed the power of words in affirmations and the use of the little voice (self-talk). At the end, a man came to me and shared his frustration concerning the lack of results he had been getting with affirmations. His relationship had gone sour and he couldn't get back on track. His life was riddled with guilt and feelings of helplessness.

I was curious about his lack of success, so I asked him how he did his affirmations. In a matter of fact way, he explained how he had, by his count, repeated his affirmation over 200,000 times with no result, each time repeating to himself (silently) a negative formulation of the desired outcome – "I will not be affected by my break up." I suggested that the negative formula was weak and the use of "not affected" was directing his subconscious to be affected. The subconscious only works on the action word, and does not recognize the negative. He agreed to change the formula, and use empowering words describing the desired state. About two weeks later, he called me, all excited about the transformation that had happened in his state of mind. He was rid of all guilt and helplessness. He was now looking forward to a new rejuvenated life.

Make It Permanent

But wishing is not enough. Because our subconscious brain is so powerful, we must ensure the permanent installation of new mental models. Just like repetition of a golf swing guided by a good instructor leads to a better trajectory and a longer drive, self-talk couched in powerful words will create a stronger impact.

Repetition creates a mental action that builds a new way of thinking. Synapses and dendrites, the parts of our brain that transmit information, get reshaped to hold a new base of thinking to deal with a behaviour or habit we want to change. The more

AÏM FOR LIFE MASTERY™

you practice, the stronger the mental model will develop. With time, it will become permanently installed. It will become an "**automatic**".

Take smoking as an example. Reframing how a person views smoking to mean a health hazard, a financial burden, a bad taste in the mouth, a bad smell on clothes, and other socially rejected aspects of smoking will lead to a belief that smoking is not part of who the person is. Without much effort, other than being diligent in doing a programming exercise, the urge to smoke will disappear. It will become an automatic. When smoke or a smoker is present, there will even be a mental rejection of the habit. That shows how the power of our subconscious brain can be harnessed to support our effort to transform how we view things.

I know how it feels. After smoking for over twenty years, I kicked the habit using this method. The automatic of rejecting cigarette smoke is now very much instilled in me. It's very real.

Repetition of a mental reframing exercise on "being a non-smoker" will install a new program that enables the bearer to interpret smoking as bad instead of not so bad. With time, the mental program will get stronger and become permanent, just like other habits we form over the course of our life. And so it is with peak performance in every other aspect of your life!

See Appendix 5 for additional notes and a recommended technique on how to reframe self-talk and program yourself for peak performance. Make your affirmations powerful and you will experience a remarkable transformation in the way you interpret things and feel about them!

AÏM FOR LIFE MASTERY™

Step Three – Seeing the Future Today

We discussed how the first step of creating peak performance through mastery was to learn to relax on command in order to enable our subconscious brain to accept new ideas.

Then we looked at how to use that preparation to dispose the brain to work on itself through the little voice, or self-talk, in order to reframe or reprogram certain mental models that affect our behaviour.

Of course, if we want to be effective and efficient, we will use powerful words to create a new perception and a new meaning for some stimuli that formerly impacted negatively on our lives.

To strengthen the ability, and quicken the process so that it takes less time to get the desired result – let's now examine another part of the technique, that of **visualization** to reinforce the desired habit or behaviour. In essence, if you use visualization, you'll increase the impact of your reframing effort to create the desired mental model.

The technique of visualization has been developed and proven for hundreds of years. It uses images to imprint the desired situation onto our subconscious brain. And therefore, you will not only talk about what you want, you will also **see** it in your mind.

Einstein once said, "Imagination is the preview of life's coming attractions." We're capable of formulating the future in our mind through pictures. Another concept that you must grasp and internalize is the fact that our subconscious brain doesn't know the difference between what is imagined and what is real.

AÏM FOR LIFE MASTERY™

You might have seen or experienced the trick of the lemon to illustrate how imagination works. A person tells you she has a lemon in her hand. She brings her hand up and opens it toward her to see the lemon. She describes it as yellow, nice and firm, feeling the juice inside, smelling so fresh. She closes her hand and squeezes the lemon, then brings the hand up to her mouth and fakes taking a big bite out of the lemon. With her sufficient exaggeration, you will have formed a pretty clear picture of the lemon. When she bites into it, you will feel the pucker in the sides of your mouth, and likely salivate as you imagine the taste. Yet, there is no lemon. It's only your imagination.

Simply put, you can make yourself believe what you want. Your subconscious brain acts on what you inject into it.

To test this statement, take a moment to recall a situation or a time when you were afraid or unsure. Somehow, you told yourself, "It's ok, everything will be fine, just relax".

In that instance you were exactly in the right programming or reframing mode to convince yourself that you had the courage or the guts to go through with the experience.

I'm thinking of a rollercoaster for some reason. There are scary moments to be concerned about when contemplating such a ride, especially if someone has described the topsy-turvy sensation you would experience before you got on it.

Visualizing an event as having already successfully happened creates the impression and the feeling that everything will be OK. Somehow, you're fooling your subconscious brain to believe that indeed, everything will be all right. Using images is a powerful tool in fooling our subconscious brain and is a great way to achieve peak performance.

AÏM FOR LIFE MASTERY™

The main reason why visualization seems to be so powerful in reframing our mind is that it uses the strongest connections between the rational and creative brains.

This very fact indicates that a reframing exercise must include visualization, the technique to view the future as if it had already happened.

This activity raises the capability to fool your subconscious brain to work toward the outcome you desire. Because it doesn't know the difference between imagined and real, it acts as a PULL to move you toward the vision you've created.

It's a wonderful ability of our subconscious brain that we should strive to consciously use to reduce the effort required to achieve peak performance and life successes in general.

Designing Performance

If we accept that it's possible to program our subconscious brain, then it's easy to accept that we can design our performance ahead of time, practice it, and deliver it at the required moment.

Sports is a good analogy. It's performance in action and under pressure because of the competitive aspect.

Back in the 1930s, a German scientist, Johannes Schultz[14], influenced by the work of Professor Oscar Vogt, formulated what is commonly known as **autogenic programming**. It was taught to East German athletes, and they went on to win more than their expected share of medals at the Olympics.

Opponents thought they were cheating since they had so many more superior performances. In the end, it was discovered that

---

[14] Shultz, Johannes Heinrich. 1884-1970. *Das Autogene Training*, 1932

they had been using mental imagery to pre-program their performance.

Autogenic programming is simply the technique of visualizing one's performance before actually performing – in other words, pre-playing the activity in one's mind. In modern times, science has been able to measure, through MRI, the brain activity associated with mental imagery. It's been shown that even though there are no physical movements, the mere act of visualizing the performance generates the same electrical impulses in the human brain that would be experienced in the actual physical performance.

The beauty of the mental rehearsal is that it can be guided to be perfect, thus establishing the brain imagery that allows peak performance under physical strain.

There are a number of recorded striking events to illustrate this concept.

Jean-Claude Killy is a French skier who had a bad leg break eight months before the 1992 Albertville Winter Olympics. His recovery prevented him from getting on skis up to two weeks prior to the competitions. Yet, he skied to a gold medal with only two weeks of alpine competition runs as compared to a whole season of competition for other entrants.

When asked how he did it, he explained that he'd been skiing the hills for eight months… in his mind. His practice runs were perfect. How could he have done badly?

Another similar experience is the story of the current senior Senator John McCain of Arizona. In 1967, he was shot down over Hanoi during a bombing mission and made a prisoner of war until his liberation in 1973.

AÏM FOR LIFE MASTERY™

When he was invited to a golf tournament in his honour just a few days after his liberation, Senator McCain played his usual score, a four handicap. People were astounded. How could he have kept his golf game so intact while in prison? The answer was simple. John McCain explained he had played eighteen holes every day that he was imprisoned – in his mind.

There were no kinks in his game. He had lost none of his ability through mental rehearsal.

If these physical performances leave you doubtful, how about the tests that were conducted on a singer at a British University? Electrodes were attached to vital points of her vocal chords, and she was asked to imagine her rehearsal without uttering a single sound. Then she actually went through a second round of practice, this time creating the melody and wonderful notes she could perform.

In both instances, the same sensory signals were produced, thus showing how the brain and its peripherals work the same way whether in an actual performance or in an imagined performance.

Of course, we shouldn't forget top level athletes in the Olympics.

If you watch skiers getting ready for their run, you'll notice how they're transfixed for a few moments before they start, eyes closed, almost flowing like in their run. Then they go down the hill as they've rehearsed.

Figure skaters do the same. And so do all athletes in different kinds of sports including golf, where the player usually sets up his ball, then takes a look down the fairway, and imagines the trajectory of his ball. The result is usually excellent if the player remains focused. Phil Mickelson is a master at it. How many times, if you've watched him, can you recall "Lefty" stopping his swing, and resetting. His focus was distracted and so, he resets the visual result to make sure his mind will guide his body.

AÏM FOR LIFE MASTERY™

Based on these stories, it becomes quite evident and believable that we can design our performance, rehearse it, and execute actions based on mental rehearsal.

It illustrates beyond the shadow of a doubt that we have the capability to create performance at will. We have the tools to do it. The challenge is to learn how to use these tools, decide what performance we want to create, and then get to work. We are indeed capable of designing our future!

Imprinting the Image

Just as a person will go to the gym repeatedly to develop strength, speed, or agility, it's important to approach mental reframing or programming in the same fashion.

As repetition is the key to develop muscle memory, so is it for mental memory.

Imprinting the image ensures that the program takes hold. Repeating the visualization exercise to install a new mental model will imprint and create new habits in your brain associated with the new thinking model. The image will become permanent, and it will be effective in proportion to the focus and attention you will attach to the details.

Practice Makes Perfect

As for any work you undertake to improve yourself, whether physically or mentally, repetition is key in creating muscle memory and gaining mastery. But unfocused or scattered repetition doesn't lead to mastery. It leads to confusion.

AÏM FOR LIFE MASTERY™

The key to mastery is to make your practice as uniform, consistent, and repeatable as possible. Thus, visualization experts such as Lee Pulos[15] recommend that you develop a mental video of what you want to accomplish. Make sure you integrate as many details as possible, using all senses to strengthen the message to your subconscious brain.

Link the details to emotions, so that your whole being gets charged up when you practice.

Repeating the video of your desired state will anchor the mental model that will soon become second nature. Within a few weeks, you'll start noticing how your new tendency or point of view, or ease of execution seems so natural. You will have gained a new habit that guides your subconscious brain to move in the desired direction without strain. You will develop a new ability that becomes second nature.

Here's a good technique that works for me.

When I want to prepare for an important meeting or presentation to a group, I take time to go and visit the place where I'll work. Then I visualize the circumstance, imagining the decor, the people, the layout of the room. I preplay the event, visualizing the screen, myself speaking, the smile on the audience's faces, the laughter where called for, the questions that will be asked, and other minute details. With time, I've gotten so good at it that the actual event is almost exactly as I imagined. And the results are usually very close to expectations. Since I practice this technique, I usually get the standing ovation I had imagined!

Making sure that your practice is the same or identical every time will bring on mastery and peak performance, and confirm the dictum that says that "perfect practice makes perfect".

---

[15] Pulos, Dr Lee. *The Power of Visualization.* Audio CD. Nightingale-Conant. 1994

AÏM FOR LIFE MASTERY™

Make sure that your practice is as structured and uniform as possible, so that you enable your subconscious brain to anchor the mental image. Once you reach that stage, it's like riding a bicycle or driving a car. It becomes second nature. The effort required for this practice will be small in comparison to the results you'll create when you have mastered peak performance.

See Appendix 6 for additional notes on visualization and a recommended technique to make your exercise fit into your mental gym process, and ensure an effective and productive practice each time you work at reprogramming your subconscious brain.

AÏM FOR LIFE MASTERY™

Step Four – Expressing Gratitude

> "…let me assert my firm belief that the only thing we have to
> fear… is fear itself – nameless, unreasoning, ….."
> **Franklin Delano Roosevelt,** 32nd United States President, inaugural speech

Here are a few thoughts about how being grateful can help us overcome fear about the future and smooth out our path toward Peak Performance

It is generally accepted that life often looks better when seen through rose-coloured glasses. Some people will argue that you can't change situations or events. It is what it is. However, if you stop and think for a moment about how you view a situation or event, it can make it look quite different.

Imagine sitting in your car, and looking ahead.

In your field of vision are the windshield and the rear-view mirror.

One fact cannot be escaped: the rear-view mirror is much smaller than the windshield itself. Now, if you integrate that fact with your driving activity, it makes sense to conclude that there is much more to see, evaluate, and assess in front of you than what you see through the rear-view mirror.

And the fact is that what's in front is more important than what is in the back when driving forward. Behind is past, and in front is yet to come.

AÏM FOR LIFE MASTERY™

So it is with life in general. Unfortunately, in life we sometimes have a tendency to look more in the rear-view mirror than in the windshield. We concentrate on the past, and forget the importance of the future. One emotion which tends to produce that effect is fear. Fear is based on past experiences that cause us to see what's coming through dark-coloured glasses.

Needless to say, if you want to free yourself to become a peak performer, you'll need to take steps to eliminate any fear barriers that stand in your way. After all, you want to work smarter, not harder. One way to move toward that goal is to eliminate fear from your mental process. Becoming adept at resetting your focus when things get clouded will free you from the unwanted emotion of fear that paralyzes you.

Gratitude Eliminates F E A R

As a first step, let's consider the following word association to reduce the stranglehold that often comes with fear.

F	false
E	evidence
A	appearing
R	real

One definition of fear can be stated as False Evidence Appearing Real (F.E.A.R.).

Indeed, fear is usually based on our apprehension of what might happen in the future. Fear may also arise if we apply the thought of an unpleasant past experience to a new experience. Another way to define it is that fear, or worry for some, can be equated to "interest paid on a loan that has yet to be taken out". In reality, there is no reason for fear since the event has not happened yet.

Martin Seligman[16] in his book "Learned Optimism" tells us how we can reduce the impact of fear of the unknown (a coming event, a potential outcome, a recognized critical moment), and its

---

[16] Seligman, Martin. *Learned Optimism*. Pocket Books. Division of Simon & Schuster. New York 1992

devastating effects, by balancing our outlook with positive self-talk. Helping our subconscious brain to recognize that there is a positive slant to the expected event or situation can provide a counterbalance to the negative, and reduce the feeling of helplessness in the face of fear.

One way to practice filling our brain activity with positive thoughts is to focus on things, people, and events for which we are **thankful**.

Take your health for example. Usually, we really appreciate the fact that we're healthy when we get sick. How about our intelligence and mental capacity? Just read about or watch people with limited mental capacity. Don't you feel privileged, happy, and get a sense of comfort when you become aware of the challenges that persons with disabilities have to face?

Looking around us, we quickly realize how easy we have it because of all the technology, tools, home features, and on and on, that make our life so easy compared to third world countries. Indeed, it's easy to find reasons to be thankful for, to express gratitude for what we have.

The trick is to make an effort once in a while to remind ourselves that we have so much to be thankful for. Thinking about it develops a positive mindset – gratitude for what we have.

This positive mindset works like good seeds in a garden. It supplies our subconscious brain with the right growth to push out the weeds of negative thinking. As a peak performer, if you sow, cultivate, and maintain the good growth, with time, you will enable your subconscious brain to push out fear, and focus only on the positive possibilities.

Since we are human and not machines, there will be times when fear will appear. But the times will be fewer and further apart. And you will empower yourself to reduce and perhaps with time, eliminate fear from your mindset. Like any other mental activity, this can be anchored and reinforced through practice.

When I was younger, starting my career as an engineer, I was afraid of what others might think about my poor English-speaking skills. It paralyzed me. I felt shy, inadequate, inferior, and hardly able to face tough situations. I was confident inside but not very good at talking with others.

However, I had one advantage which helped me eliminate that fear. I hung on to the fact that I could speak both English and French, which the people I worked with could not. With time, and repeated moments of gratefulness for my double ability, I conquered my fear. Today, I facilitate, speak, and coach in both languages, and my English is nearly flawless.

Make It Part of Your Mental Gym

As with any part of the peak performance recipe, you'll want gratitude to become a habit, an automatic response that supports and assists your efforts in creating peak performance in your life.

Therefore, like going to the gym to develop your physical muscles, you'll want to strengthen your brain connections through repeated gratefulness. It is recommended that the gratitude exercise be added to your process for peak performance. Once the relaxation, affirmations, and visualizations are done, the moment of gratitude should be added as another moment of practice.

An effective method is to think about 4-5 reasons for being thankful at this very moment. It should be different from the last practice, and it should be kept simple. Just like affirmations, gratitude should be expressed with words that resonate and uplift you.

AÏM FOR LIFE MASTERY™

Here's how I express my gratitude in these moments. For example, I focus on my family and thank God for the healthy and intelligent children I have. I'm also thankful for their ability to lead good lives. I express gratitude for the opportunity to have them in my life, in good and bad times, to listen to their opinions. And I'm thankful for the pride they have bestowed upon me as their father.

It doesn't take much time, and this moment of gratitude acts as a reminder of the wonderful life I have. It strengthens my desire to make a difference for those around me. I have no fear!

So reflect, describe, and feel the reasons for being grateful at this moment – these can be flowers, the smell of coffee, good kids, a wonderful partner, parents who took care of you, good friends, the abilities you particularly cherish, etc., etc.

Make sure that you think about these reasons for gratitude with feeling. Live the sensation strongly throughout your body. Enjoy the fact that these things, events or persons you're thankful for help you see things in a positive way with rosy glasses, and contribute to eliminate fear in your life!

Count Your Blessings

Counting your blessings will occupy your mind and anchor the reasons to be positive in your thinking at a subconscious level.

Too often, we forget all the good that surrounds us. How fortunate we are gets clouded by all the bad news that is splashed across the newspapers, the internet, radio and TV. Because news is entertainment, and humans have a fascination for the morbid, at times, it seems that the media is colluding to create an atmosphere of powerlessness, disillusionment, and downright sense of "what's the use?".

The truth is that if we want to perform at the peak of our abilities and beyond, we must cut through the veil of negativity. We must help ourselves be the best that we can be. Counting our blessings somehow acts as a counterbalance to external forces, and reduces the paralysis caused by fear.

Keeping Your Ego in Check

Too often, we let our ego take over, and that leads us to believe that we deserve better, that we have a right to be spared, that we should not have to suffer the impact of all this stuff that produces fear on a large scale. A recommended reading on the subject of Ego is Wayne Dyer's book "The Shift: Taking Your Life from Ambition to Meaning"[17].

There are times when it's difficult to maintain a clear focus and minimize the burden of fear generated by external influences. We let our ego get in the way. Questions like: "What about my needs?" "Why should I give up my opinion?" "How do you think I will feel if I surrender?" "What's left to make me feel good?"

At times, we need to take drastic action to knock ourselves back into reality. One way to do this is through "Wally's Eyes".

Wally Kozak is a remarkable man I've known for many years. He's a tremendous coach, philosopher, profound thinker, and a good friend and mentor. We're very much on the same level of thinking, read the same

> **Wally's Eyes**
> ☹ - sad
> ☺ - happy

books, and our effort is very focused on enabling people to find their gift (as he calls it). The gift refers to the experience, expertise, abilities, skills and knowledge that a person has accumulated over his or her lifetime.

Let me explain what I mean by "Wally's Eyes".

---

[17] Dyer, Wayne W. *The Shift: Taking Your Life from Ambition to Meaning.* Hay House. 2010

AÏM FOR LIFE MASTERY™

Wally has studied, developed, and applied a technique to teach people how to believe in the power of their inner brain action. It's been applied for many years to business as well as with sports performers, at minor levels as well as with pros and even Olympic athletes.

"Wally's Eyes" are the expressions illustrated by the icons commonly seen on the internet, and particularly in messenger software (or social media) to express a state of emotions (they're called emoticons).

"Wally's Eyes" are the smiling eyes and the sad eyes found in these emoticons. He uses these two figures to illustrate how what we see impacts our internal state of mind – that of being powerless, or powerful. To illustrate the point, Wally uses an exercise where a person is asked to pair up with another, stand side by side facing each other. One person raises an arm to a horizontal position at the shoulder. The other places a hand on the extended arm at the wrist. Then Wally asks the person with the raised arm to look at the emoticons in turn, starting with the smiling one. The other person is asked to press down on the arm. When the person looks at the smiling face, the arm is strong. But when the person is shown the sad face, the arm can barely be kept up, and it takes little force to push it down.

Try this test with a person you trust. You'll be struck by the effect that a simple picture can have to empower you, or make you weak. You will never be able to discount the impact of what you see or say to yourself ever again.

Remember! Your subconscious brain doesn't know the difference between what is real and what is imagined. Be careful of the ideas or images you let roam in your mind. They can either empower you, or make you helpless.

So it is with peak performance. Be alert! Recognize the moment! Think about Wally's Eyes. Learn to move away from fear (on

AÏM FOR LIFE MASTERY™

automatic) by expressing gratitude. You'll see your life through rose-coloured glasses! And that is empowering!

Keep the Faith

> "There is but one cause of human failure. And that is man's lack of faith in his true Self."
> — **William James,**
> psychologist and author

Finally, if you want your self-talk to be effective, the more details you can provide to clarify the picture (your brain works better with pictures), the more you'll be able to create strong mental models. Especially when expressing gratitude, be sure to provide your brain with solid information that it can bite into so that it will quickly move to a place where fear has no room to flourish.

Just keep in mind that emotions tend to make us blind. Eliminating fear is an activity that can help launch and sustain your journey to excellence and peak performance.

With no unwanted negative emotions to cloud the picture, you'll generate a stronger drive toward your goal, and you'll free yourself of the cloak of doubt that tends to drop on you when you're not sure of the result. Believe and you will see it![18]

---

[18] Dyer, Wayne W. *You'll See IT When You Believe It.* Harper Paperbacks. 2001.

AÏM FOR LIFE MASTERY™

Step Five – Creating Mastery

In sequence, you've learned to relax and master your brain activity, then in a relaxed state, to inject new thoughts into your subconscious through affirmations (the little voice), and to anchor these thoughts at the mental level with visualization, so that peak performance becomes permanent. We then bonded the new mental state through the practice of expressing gratitude. With FEAR reduced and even eliminated, negative emotions will have little impact on your focus.

It's now time to examine the **M** in **AïM**. It was great to develop awareness, internalize this concept and start integrating it into your daily routine. However, what you really want is to make this a habit, a second nature approach to applying **the right stuff, in the right amount, at the right time**™.

It takes a structured and disciplined approach to ensure a uniform, consistent, and repeatable process that guarantees peak performance "….every time, all the time, forever" (Bill Conway, TQM Master, Deming Principles[19]).

Practice, Practice, Practice – The Mental Gym

Talk to any high performing person, in business, sports or in everyday life. If you ask them, "What makes you so good, so outstanding in your field?" you'll hear something to the effect that

---

[19] Deming, William Edwards. Read about Deming and his 14 Key Principles in Wikipedia

AÏM FOR LIFE MASTERY™

they are focused, apply a certain discipline to their approach, and …. They practice all the time, in any way, shape or form possible.

Woody Hayes, the famous coach of the Ohio State University Football Buckeyes (1951-1978; record of 205 wins and 61 losses) was famous for this quote, "You're either getting better, or you're getting worse". He knew how a feeling of having reached the peak was a trap for defeat in the long run. His philosophy reaches deep into our hearts – if you want to succeed, you must keep working at your skill.

Thus, as in any other endeavour, mastery of your abilities can only survive and thrive if you learn to practice, practice, practice.

As for the physical aspect of performance, where one goes to the gym to strengthen muscles and keep suppleness and agility ever present, the maintenance of the mental capability developed through awareness, internalization, integration and practice, must be sustained through constant focus and targeted repetition.

The best way to ensure that the mental gym becomes part of who you are, is to make it part of your daily living. Schedule it so that you don't forget. Consider it as important as food and water to sustain your physical body. Make it a must in any circumstance. Learn to maintain your mental agility and strength.

Vince Lombardi, famous football coach of the Green Bay Packers used to say, "Fatigue makes cowards of us all."

Take proactive action to always be in shape (that is, mental shape) to master your thinking process, so that you never tire out at the most inappropriate moment. If you get tired mentally, you'll have a tendency to become a "coward" and shy away from delivering your best effort.

The end result will be regret, and that's not what you want to settle for.

AÏM FOR LIFE MASTERY™

Plan, Plan, Plan

It's said that "Those who fail to plan usually plan to fail".

Life is a series of events, many of them unexpected. If you're to succeed in accomplishing what you set out to do, you must have a plan. Nothing gets done successfully without one.

Just think of eating. If you want to be healthy, and provide your body with nourishing food, you must plan your menu, put money aside to buy the food, go buy the ingredients, and prepare the meals accordingly. Otherwise, you're leaving your physical health to chance.

With respect to peak performance, the same rule applies.

You must plan your activities so that time is set aside for the process to be practiced DAILY. I'm not kidding. You'll want to develop a habit of mentally practicing. Otherwise, it's easy to derail the process, forget about practicing, and ultimately torpedo your own effort to install peak performance.

It depends on motivation of course. But is it not worth taking the steps to make your life journey the best possible?

I encourage you to make space for your mental practice. Make life easier by planning your steps along the way. Make sure that you take care of the important stuff, the things that help you bring out the best in you. Be sure to go to your mental gym in your daily schedule.

Do, Do, Do

It can appear to be repetitious, but then, repetition is the key to mastery.

Therefore, it's not only important to focus and decide on what you will do to make yourself a peak performer, but it's an obligation to

AÏM FOR LIFE MASTERY™

yourself and others around you to do what's required to implement peak performance.

A useful concept to remember is that "to every action, there is an equal and opposite reaction". This is an irrefutable law of physics that is at work in

> As an old Chinese proverb says:
> I **hear** and I forget,
> I **see** and I remember,
> I **do** and I understand.

the physical as well as the mental realms. This law supports the belief that if you do, you will produce results. Nike was surely applying this concept when they adopted their slogan "Just do it".

There may be days when you will doubt the value of the effort you put in to create mental habits that allow you to use **the right stuff, in the right amount, at the right time**™. Be assured that if you respect diligently the concept of "do, do, do", there will be a reaction. If you keep focused on the process and do what you have planned to do, the results will follow.

With time, constant awareness, and sustained practice, you will reach peak performance. It will become a habit. Then you'll recognize and understand the impact of having **the right stuff, in the right amount, at the right time**™. Second nature will help you to make the right choice in most circumstances. Your neural networks will take over and you will experience the expansion of peak performance into areas where you thought improvement would never be possible.

Biological Neural Networks

While I'm not an expert at the complexities of the neurochemical regulation of memory, I do know that knowledge transfer in our brains is the direct result of the natural ability of our subconscious brain to apply anchored knowledge in areas that are outside the realm of our consciousness.

AÏM FOR LIFE MASTERY™

For example, in the case of weight control, without thinking about it, biological neural networks that contain a structured and disciplined approach for dealing effectively with frustrating situations at work, may transfer through the neurological pathways to the way that our appetite and weight are controlled.

As if by magic, better balance is installed in our eating habits and we maintain weight effectively.

This is just an example. Subconsciously, we experience the benefits of peak performance in situations in which we've never made an attempt to develop emotional control. This ability is transferred through neural networks to different parts of our brain. This happens throughout our daily lives.

In a very simplistic way, biological neural networks are the clusters of brain cells composed of neurons (electrically excitable cells that process and transmit information by electrical and chemical signalling) from which extend multiple dendrites (little branches that act as receivers), and their attached axons which send electrical impulses to surrounding neurons through their branching network called synapses (emitters).

When a signal moves through an axon down to its synapses which interact with neighbouring dendrites, a knowledge transfer occurs. According to researchers in the field, even though the concept cannot be well explained or reproduced, it has been recognized as the pathway through which the brain learns.

Since all the brain cells are lumped together in this mass of grey matter between our ears, we can count on this natural capability in our journey toward peak performance. If you'd like more information on this fascinating subject, I'd recommend a Wikipedia definition for an abbreviated explanation of the mechanism and how it works. Type in "neural networks".

AÏM FOR LIFE MASTERY™

We've arrived at the last stage of the peak performance process. Everything you've constructed so far is now ready to be wrapped up into a neat package. You will want to call upon that performance package to provide the PULL and the guidance in any given situation in your life. You will want to have quick access to the subconscious abilities you've anchored that have now become second nature.

Stepping Into Peak Performance

To anchor peak performance into your everyday habits, let's examine a principle of psycho-cybernetics[20] (more recently defined by Neuro Linguistic Programming) to turn the whole process into a powerful trigger. By trigger, we mean a quick, almost instantaneous means of getting into your peak performance state. That is the state where the benefits of relaxation, affirmation, visualization, gratitude, and practice all come together to make you a powerful and capable performer who can effectively take on any challenge coming your way!

The idea is to create mental imagery to move you at will from a place of rest to a place of performance.

The expression "stepping into your circle of performance" is used to provide a distinctive movement that describes the action linked to the passage from relaxation to activation. The "circle" image is to cast a shape on the state that is never-ending, continuous, and holistic. A circle has no beginning, no middle, no end. It's "into" or "out of" providing a clear distinction of the place where you will be in a state of peak performance.

---

[20] Summer, Bobbe, Ph.D. with Falstein, Mark. *Psycho-Cybernetics 2000*. Prentice-Hall, NJ. 2000

AÏM FOR LIFE MASTERY™

Neuro Linguistic Programming (NLP)

In order to use this tool effectively, it's useful to have a simple understanding of how this concept works. In my own layman terms, I offer a summarized description. Much has been written about the subject. If you care to find out more, I have included references that you might want to consult.

Neuro Linguistic Programming™ (NLP™) is defined as the study of the structure of subjective experience (our mental models built over years of living, all the experiences of daily life). People such as Virginia Satir, Milton Erickson and Fritz Perls[21] have had amazing results with their clients over time using behaviour structure patterns to help them understand their undesirable habits and create new thinking pathways that allow them to regain control of their lives.

Using these structures, Richard Bandler[22] along with John Grinder[23] (co-inventors of NLP) developed models to create new ways of understanding how verbal and non-verbal communication affect the human brain. These models present us with the opportunity to learn how to gain more control over the automatic functions of our own neurology (thinking). NLP can also help to communicate better with others around us.

---

[21] Satir, Virginia; Erikson, Milton and Perls, Fritz. Experts in the field of cognitive behaviour modification

[22] **Richard Wayne Bandler** (born February 24, 1950) is an American author and trainer in alternative psychology and self-help. He is best known as the co-inventor (with John Grinder) of Neuro Linguistic programming (NLP), a collection of concepts and techniques intended to understand and change human behavior patterns. He also developed other systems known as Design Human Engineering (DHE) and Neuro Hypnotic Repatterning (NHR).

[23] **John Grinder** Ph.D. (born January 10, 1940) is an American linguist, author, management consultant, trainer and speaker.

AÏM FOR LIFE MASTERY™

To explain simply, NLP is a technique that anyone can apply to modify unwanted behaviours or create new behaviours using techniques that speak to the nervous system.

The signs of how NLP works are all around us.

For example, you taste some new food and find it delicious. Next thing you know, whenever that food is mentioned, you salivate at the thought of eating it again. You've been programmed. Or in the visual sense, you see an accident happening and from then on, you're a bit queasy when you find yourself in that same spot. Through the visual sensory stimulus, you've been programmed to fear this particular place. The same applies for sound, touch and smell. Once you've smelled smoke, you immediately think "fire". Those are examples of behaviour structure patterns that regulate our responses (automatic) in different situations.

The principle is normal and easily understandable. We live it every day of our life. The big deal is that once we recognize that this process is always going on, we can use it to program ourselves. We can develop the ability to have predictable and helpful reactions in certain challenging situations.

Installing the Circle

Using the NLP concept of creating mental models, it's now possible to establish a model to consolidate and regroup all the various stages of the peak performance cycle you've learned. As our senses are like keyboards on a computer, the key is to link the knowledge and abilities stored in the mental practice of relaxation, affirmations, visualization, expressing gratitude and repetition into one powerful mental image.

The technique suggested, based on research by experts in the field, is to create a mental image of a Circle of Performance.

AÏM FOR LIFE MASTERY™

The circle is where all the benefits of the steps you've practiced are stored, ready to be called upon. The fruits of relaxation, affirmations, visualization, gratitude and repetition are ready to be put into action on a moment's notice. They are part of you. They've become an automatic response that is ready to be put to work when needed!

Installation Steps

The way to install peak performance is to first set yourself into a quiet mode, something you've learned through relaxation with the **3R Process**©.

Close your eyes, and imagine your Circle of Performance sitting on the ground just beside you. In it are all the skills, knowledge, abilities and desire to perform that you've practiced during your long series of mental exercises at your mental gym.

Feel the power, the energy, the drive, the confidence, and the belief in your ability that comes from focusing on the circle. Experience the transformation that happens inside your body as you focus more and more on the possibilities that the circle creates for you. When you feel warm inside and ready to launch, physically take a sideways step into your Circle of Performance. You are now in state, in the zone, in flow, fully equipped to meet your next challenge.

As for all the aspects of the peak performance process, this mental exercise is to be repeated, practiced, and locked in with a physical movement in order to lock it into your mental models' storage bin. It is recommended that you practice stepping into your Circle of Performance every time you do a mental gym session (every day!!!).

AÏM FOR LIFE MASTERY™

With practice it will become second nature (automatic). Just closing your eyes, imagining the circle, feeling the power invade your body, then repeatedly stepping into the Circle of Performance will ultimately result in competency in your technique.

Once your mental model gets anchored (after 20-30 days), you'll be able to trigger yourself into a state or zone where you can perform at the peak of your ability. With time, you will like to step into your Circle of Performance because it will transform how you feel in a flash!

With time, you will also develop the urge to call on your Circle, not all the time, but in moments when you really need to do **the right thing, in the right amount, at the right time**™! In those moments when you feel you have to perform at your best, you'll have the ability to relax and rise to the situation. You will have mastered your performance on command.

Testimonial of a Master Coach

Wally Kozak has been involved with peak performance for many years. Among his extensive involvements with high level performing athletes, he was with the Canadian National Women's Hockey Team who won the gold medal in Salt Lake City at the 2002 Winter Olympics. After he had read the description of the installation process above, he had the following comments:

> "Interesting how this concept parallels the 2002 National Women's Olympic preparation routine which included an autogenic session having the players relax and be reminded of how we were so well prepared to "peak perform" and be "our best" during the final game. This session provided the foundation needed to play well.

AÏM FOR LIFE MASTERY™

Outcomes were never mentioned, only how well prepared we were to deal with anything and everything technically and emotionally in the final game.

We had followed the 3R Process to a T. This process was applied formally through the season and it had a major impact on maintaining an 'ideal performance state'. It was … the right stuff, the right amount and the right time. Relaxation, affirmation, visualization, and gratitude were reinforced at the right time bearing the fruits needed for Peak Performance."

Key Points to Remember

In order to install peak performance in an effective and productive way, there must be a systematic and structured approach in place to ensure a uniform, consistent and reliable method. The approach consists of six steps. Any step that is omitted can mess up your effort and produce less than the expected results.

* Step 1 –
  Quieting the brain: preparing the ground (brain cells) so that it is adaptive and malleable in order to receive the commands you will send to it in the steps that follow.

* Step 2 –
  Reframing Self-talk: learning to guide your internal talk to create new thinking pathways that will support the new desired behaviours; developing a strong affirmation technique.

* Step 3 –
  Seeing the future today: in order to create a bright future, it pays to design it and see it as a vision. Make sure it contains the details that drive your subconscious brain to PULL you toward

the desired results. You've learned to visualize your outcomes in a way that helps create new thinking pathways to peak performance.

- Step 4 –
  Expressing Gratitude: not only is it necessary to build a strong process to install new thinking pathways, but it is also fundamental to remove your natural tendency of letting fear of the unknown interfere with your drive to peak performance. Make sure the effort is minimized by removing the F E A R barriers to your best performance. Look at things through a positive lens.

- Step 5 –
  Creating mastery: as all top performers know, the secret to peak performance is mastery. And as top performers have shown over time, the key to mastery is practice. You now have a recipe to anchor mastery. You can design your repetitions to create an automatic response in moments of challenge.

- Step 6 –
  Anchoring Peak Performance: the final step ensures that you can get in a peak performance state at will by creating a trigger for quick access. The trigger consolidates every step into one key signal that puts your subconscious brain into action at the desired moment. Now that you have learned the trigger, you can be a peak performer on command, just as the Canadian National Women's Hockey Team demonstrated at the 2002 Winter Olympics in Salt Lake City, USA.

AÏM FOR LIFE MASTERY™

PART IV - RELEASING YOUR BRAKES

STAYING ON TRACK...

AÏM FOR LIFE MASTERY™

Removing Barriers to Performance

> "Man is free at the moment he wishes to be."
> — **Voltaire,** French writer, historian, and philosopher

Now that you have the recipe to create peak performance, the next step is to make it easier to achieve this state by removing existing barriers in your thinking pathways. Naturally, you will want to free yourself of these barriers so that you can perform in most circumstances at your chosen level of excellence, closer to the peak of your abilities.

Here's an example of a common barrier that can reduce the impact of the best techniques you've learned.

A person is called upon to make a business presentation to top level management. She has expert knowledge and understanding of the subject. She can deliver a concept on the spot without preparation. Yet, when she finds out to whom the presentation will be made, she gets really stressed out and almost gets sick because she is not used to going in front of top management. Her great assurance vanishes. She feels almost incapable of thinking. Her belief is that since she has never done it for them, she will mess up. Fear of the unknown paralyzes her. She lets her emotions cloud her solid knowledge of the subject. It is a debilitating feeling which renders her helpless.

The fact is that if she relaxes, and steps back to remember other instances where she has delivered a similar piece of work, she will remember that she received nothing but accolades for her performance. She is indeed capable of a high level performance but she lets her emotions create a seemingly insurmountable barrier. Her thinking that she is inadequate rules her mind. It can potentially torpedo her performance.

I encourage you to take a closer look at the barriers in the following pages. Some of them could make or break your effort to build peak performance into your daily routine.

You might ask why I held back on these important barriers to your success until now. I felt that until you fully understood the concept of peak performance, it may have been overwhelming to discuss undesired mental models (paradigms) and their related emotional states.

Applying peak performance (**the right stuff, in the right amount, at the right time™**) will be more easily achieved if you make sure that barriers to implementation are reduced or eliminated. To gain maximum advantage of this new recipe, please pay attention to tendencies that could torpedo your efforts to create peak performance. I'm talking here about inherent or natural barriers to your newfound awareness. Let's focus on removing a few of these barriers.

Maximizing Your Effort

This chapter should be read and reread, digested, tested, assimilated, and put into practice so that your effort to install peak performance is not held back by invisible forces which are continually at work.

These invisible forces are called your natural tendencies to resist change. They've been organized into four distinct barriers to peak performance – disruptive mental models, unfocused communication, runaway emotions, and random decision-making. To help you steer the course, a few thoughts on measuring progress have been added as a fifth part. After all, if you don't measure, how will you know if you are progressing on your journey to peak performance?

AÏM FOR LIFE MASTERY™

Let's discuss each one and make an effort to link the explanations to your reality.

My goal is to take you from the known to the unknown, help you unlearn and relearn, remove these barriers, and install a recognition and rectification system of some of the thinking pathways that may interfere with your work to create peak performance. Enjoy the ride!

AÏM FOR LIFE MASTERY™

The Paradigm Shifts – Changing Gears

You might ask, "What are paradigms?" Simply, they are mental models (thinking pathways) built on education, experiences, upbringing, exposure to important people in our life, or any event which have marked us emotionally. They occupy a special place in our subconscious mind and in most cases, provide the framework and reference points for our deliberate actions, or in crisis situations, our automatic response – fight or flight.

We tend to revert to primitive reaction in tense situations, unless we learn to **AiM** to gain some measure of mastery.

So, what are we to do?

The answer lies in transforming some of our paradigms (mental models or thinking pathways) to enable us to make good choices in our continued effort to seek peak performance (**the right stuff, in the right amount, at the right time**™).

We want to change a certain way of thinking so that our automatic reaction will be improved to become a support or help in our journey to peak performance. We will change a paradigm from being a barrier to performance to being an asset in creating peak performance.

Over the years, I've gained the belief and understanding of what I consider to be the most important barriers to peak performance: rigidity, necessity, judging, blaming, complaining, scattered thinking, and liking. In my mind, I submit that changing (or shifting) some or all of these seven paradigms will further enable you to become a peak performer.

AÏM FOR LIFE MASTERY™

The concept is simple. But it takes hard work, determination, patience, persistence, and continuous focus to produce the shifts and remove these significant barriers. As was explained in the implementation of the peak performance steps, you have to **AïM** for life mastery if you're to be successful.

Making the Shift Work for You

As noted, the seven barriers described can form the backdrop of your paradigm shift to peak performance. Each will be reviewed briefly to start you thinking about how you can make it happen for you.

Different people will find different challenges associated with these paradigms. Each one of us comes from a different place: different parents, different teachers, different culture, different growing experiences, mental capabilities and tendencies. In a word, we're all different. That's good! You must make it work for you.

Paradigm Shift 1:   from rigid to flexible
In no particular order, the first paradigm shift involves our innate resistance to change.

We have a tendency to be rigid, to face change with a certain amount of negativity. We're creatures of habit. Anything that seems to change our anchored habits goes against our natural tendency and feels uncomfortable. As Horace Mann, a 19th century American education reformer, once said, "Habit is a cable; we weave a thread of it each day, and at last we cannot break it."

In our modern day society, change is the norm. Nothing stays constant for long. Therefore, in order to increase our ability to face challenges effectively and effort-lessly, we should be flexible, ride with the tide, accept "different" as a positive way of life. Otherwise, we will waste a lot of energy resisting changes that are out of our control. Peak performance is about minimizing effort to produce greater results.

Paradigm Shift 2: from necessity to possibility

It's important to remember that we don't need anything except the air that we breathe to stay alive. Over the years, we've learned the mental model of need (necessity), and it doesn't serve us very well. You may disagree, but remember, this is about peak performance, and peak performance cannot be based on some imaginary constraint.

If we're to be able to release our energy to produce maximum results, we must use an approach that is empowering. Saying that we "need" is compulsive and creates a limitation. There might indeed be a constraint, but for anyone who wants to deal effectively with the situation, it's much better to talk about "want" which propels you because it is based on personal choice. So, necessity (need) can be replaced with choice (want) to enable us to use personal power freely. And choice means endless possibilities which free us from imaginary constraints.

Paradigm Shift 3: from judging to evaluating

We've been taught from an early age to judge. It's in line with our natural tendency to simplify and reduce issues to a manageable level. In learning to judge, we learned to disregard the in-between options or possibilities. It's either black or white, good or bad, high or low. And this is good, since it allows us to make sense of the multitude of inputs we deal with every second of our waking life. However, this capability also limits our ability to see all aspects of a situation. And consequently, we sometimes make abstraction of useful information that could lead to a better result.

AÏM FOR LIFE MASTERY™

The trick is to learn to evaluate a situation, fact or statement. From the Latin "ex" – e (out of, from), the word "evaluate" indicates that extracting value from a fact or situation will lead to a more accurate consideration. That should result in a more effective point of view, a more appropriate understanding, and in the end, a more useful conclusion because we've explored the various angles. In peak performance, we stress the right stuff. Judging can restrain our ability to get the right stuff, and thus, we end up with a less than desirable opinion, decision, or direction.

Paradigm Shift 4:   from blaming to helping
This one is especially hard to accept. Since we were babies, we heard blame being thrown around. After all, isn't this a popular sport? We blame the government, the law, the education system, the health system, the management, the hoodlums, the rich, the poor, and on, and on. We've been weaned on "blame".

But as for other habits, if we're to produce peak performance, blame is not going to be one of the choice tools! Rather, shifting to a perspective of helping will at least empower us to take command. Blame makes us weak. A will to help makes us strong because it is a personal choice. And helping is one of the natural inclinations of humankind. Don't you think that following a natural instinct would be easier than pointing a finger? Is it not the mindset you want to create for a more successful and happy life?

Paradigm Shift 5:   from complaining to problem-solving
Another well-learned habit that stops us dead in our tracks is complaining. Have you ever found yourself muttering under your breath because someone is doing something that is not proper? If you stop and think back, how many times for example have you deplored the fact that your municipal council is wasting your tax dollars? Or better yet, how about the curses you shout out when

the snow plough passes through after you've cleared your driveway entrance? Even in small things, how about the toothpaste tube not being capped properly? Or the food not being warm enough? Or the dog chewing on your shoe?

It's been proven through research that negative thoughts alter our metabolic function, and cause secretion of bad hormones that make you weak. Complaining is one such brain activity that leaves you weak. Because complaining is usually negative. It draws attention to an unwanted behaviour, thing or situation that creates a negative state of emotion. I'm sure that this does not sound foreign to you. If you stop and take time to feel how complaining saps your energy, you will quickly seek to change the approach.

One technique that's very positive and can help create forward-looking action is problem-solving.

I know, I know. You'll tell me that you can't solve every problem around you. Proposition granted. It's just that thinking habits are easy to form and they become our guides in many instances. Remember Gandhi's words. If you develop the habit of taking a problem-solving approach when things go wrong instead of complaining, you will develop a positive outlook on life. A positive outlook creates secretion of good hormones, the kind that powers you up and allows you to reach peak performance.

Paradigm Shift 6: from scattered to focused
In this day and age, we must work hard to stay in good mental shape. Things happen so fast that sometimes we wonder where time went. Even worse, we wonder how we can get it all done. Multi-tasking has become the word of the day.

Just look around when travelling along city streets or taking the bus, or waiting at the airport, the bank, the supermarket. Many people are hooked on their cell phone, yakking away while doing something else. How about the law having to be enacted to reduce accidents due to cell phone distraction in the car? We've become a society regimented by speed. Everything must be done yesterday.

Now, I can't argue against that. It is what it is. Speed has taken over. Gone are the days when we went to church with the horse and buggy. I know that dates me, but perhaps, it's more indicative of the massive changes we've witnessed in the last 50-60 years. Speed has become a necessity in information transfer. We've gone global. Time barriers have been broken down. And if we're to compete, we must speed up!!

There is still a limit to our ability to perform when things speed up. We have not yet learned to go at nanosecond speed like a computer. Modern technology appears to be multi-tasking. However, it's an illusion. A computer does only one thing at a time, but at lightning speed.

As humans, we can't do that.

So, the answer is to focus. If you want to apply peak performance in your daily routine, you have to learn to be focused. Your brain has not been trained yet to change focus as quickly as a computer does. To apply the right stuff, in the right amount, at the right time, you must focus. Scattered will not do.

Paradigm Shift 7:   from liking to loving
So much has been written and said about love that we've come to totally misunderstand the concept. At least, that's my opinion. We're bombarded by commercials, movies, books, the internet and many other media with ideas that give us a false appreciation of love.

AÏM FOR LIFE MASTERY™

As eminent psychologist Denis Waitley[24] states, "Love is not looking at each other, but looking in the same direction together". Think about it. We've grown with the thought that love is the touchy feely state that we feel toward a fellow human being when the chemistry of personalities mixes up well. We give it attributes that cloud the real definition that can empower us.

Love is the powerful emotion that enables a person to do things beyond expectation because it involves full engagement..

Love is steady, eternal, bonding, soothing, forgiving... You're free to add whatever qualifier you want to choose. **Just remember that love doesn't exist if there isn't a common goal**. In the long run, just looking at each other will not cut it. There must be more. Looking at each other fades, loses strength, and becomes boring. There must be something else.

You say, "What's he talking about?" I would submit that, if you take a step back, and deep down inside, reflect on what love is for you, you'll soon realize that attraction to another person is superficial, flimsy, and weakens when bad things happen. That's called liking. Liking is a preference. It can change according to circumstances. There is no real commitment. In interpersonal relationships, just think of the times you've been hot for someone, then grew cold when another person of interest showed up, or the subject of your liking did something you didn't appreciate!

Love is commitment. You may think commitment to another person when it comes to relationship. But in reality, don't you think that love is a commitment to a goal you have bought into, dedicated yourself to reaching, a result that you made mandatory for your life to be fulfilled? The other person happened to want to walk with you in that direction, and decided to equally commit. Yes, feelings and emotions come out of that exercise. After all, we're not machines but feeling human beings.

---

[24] Waitley, Denis. Author, trainer, psychologist and producer of numerous self-help books.

AÏM FOR LIFE MASTERY™

It's just that we need to recognize what love really is if we are to make full use of the power that love generates. For peak performance, it's beneficial to shift from liking to loving, from preference to commitment.

Peak performance is loving and committing to a journey of excellence every day of your life.

AÏM FOR LIFE MASTERY™

Communication Barriers

Since 1985, I've been studying communications and its impact on peak performance.

Back then, I remember research that talked about communication and knowledge being the key ingredients to success. The people looking into the concept were reporting that in most business contexts, success was due to about 75% communication skills and 25% knowledge. It made a lot of sense to me. As an engineer working with a multi-national company since 1972, I had concluded that indeed, knowledge was not the master key to success. All around me, people with much less knowledge were getting ahead. The reason? They either had a natural ability to communicate or had mastered the skill over time.

In my awakening to the fact, I studied the books and soon became aware that research did not lie. Indeed, communication skills played the biggest part in the success of entrepreneurs. Over the years, I've developed training modules, coached professionals, and continued to observe people around me. The same scenario plays out again and again. Those who are gifted with good communication skills or have developed the skill are doing much better than the others.

> "You can have brilliant ideas, but if you cannot get them across, your ideas will not get you anywhere."
> — **Lee Iacocca,**
> Businessman, author, former CEO of Chrysler Corporation

Now, you might ask, "why is that?"

The fact is that no amount of knowledge is really useful if it is not communicated properly. In fact, current research shows that success in business is due to over 90% communication skills; it's mind boggling when you stop and think about it. It can even be maddening. The reality is that statistics don't lie… and that the lack of good communication skills can be a huge barrier to your peak performance.

Communications is a vast subject and takes on different aspects depending on the different possibilities of human interactions.

Refer to Appendix 7 for concepts and techniques that can help you to remove a few barriers on your journey to peak performance.

Here are a couple of reflections to anchor the big picture for you. Become and stay aware of your communication style and you will certainly reduce some of the barriers that can hinder your progress on the road to excellence.

Communication to Self

The biggest barrier to peak performance in our day to day life is our **self-talk**. In an unconscious way, we continually block our progress by the things we tell ourselves.

Just sit still for a moment, don't move, don't think, just let your mind roam.

It takes little time for a whirlwind of thoughts to surge into your conscious mind, doesn't it? It just happens. Why you say? Well, when you stop driving and directing your thinking activity, your subconscious brain continues to work – it's like on a flywheel. The momentum never stops, if you don't stop it. Thoughts race through your mind a mile a minute. And depending on your state at the moment (sad, happy, angry, depressed, etc.), a barrage of thoughts will appear, and your little voice will go to work. If you let it continue, pretty soon, depending on your emotional state, you will be sliding down the spiral of despair, or rising in the sky of your desires. It's a continuous process that goes on whether you like it or not!

Now, in peak performance, you want to liberate your potential, enable yourself to guide your energy, minimize waste, and maximize results.

What will you do to ensure that the little voice is helping you (most of the time)? In peak performance, it's important to master your thought process by programming your brain.

Programming! Doesn't that sound like brainwashing?

Well, we can always make things sound the way we want. I would suggest that the word "brainwashing" is an oxymoron. It's not helpful, and leads to suspicion and helplessness. More powerful and definitely empowering would be to refer to "creating new thinking pathways". That's what commercials do. They incite you to buy. If you look into it, you will find that marketing efforts are supported by psychological research on the workings of the human brain.

If the concept works that way for marketing purposes, why not use it to our advantage to imprint good thinking pathways on our subconscious brain in order to reach Peak Performance?

Communicating to yourself can be a powerful way to achieve peak performance. It takes focus and, as with everything else, practice. The technique is called "affirmations and visualization mental programming" and it's easy to apply. You've already learned how to do it. The key is to follow a systematic, structured, and sustained process to imprint a new mental pathway that will cause your subconscious brain to change how it interprets what is really going on.

An example might be the action taken to stop smoking.

AÏM FOR LIFE MASTERY™

If you've gone through the effort, you know it's not easy. Unless you attach particular focus to a transformation in thinking, you will not succeed. You can shout all day that you don't want to smoke; it won't work if you don't prepare yourself to receive the message. It will also be difficult if you don't use powerful words, and if you don't see yourself as a non-smoker.

The self-image needs to be changed. Mental programming helps to achieve such a goal. Remember, it takes 20-30 days to install a new thinking pathway, and recall requires repetition, repetition, repetition.

Apply the programming technique to your self-communication so that you effect a change in the words you use. You want to make sure that how you talk to yourself will provide strength to your resolve, and positive attitude in your behaviour.

As your self-talk reflects what you're thinking, beware that you don't act as a destructive force on your journey to peak performance.

> "The worst lies are the lies we tell ourselves. We live in denial of what we do, even what we think. We do this because we're afraid.. "
> **- Richard Bach.** author and writer

It would be terribly disappointing to do a lot of the work already discussed, and end up sabotaging the outcome by negative or destructive self-talk!

You will do well to become attuned to the words you use when talking to yourself.

Awareness of this should create an approach that aligns with your goals and enables you to progress as fast as possible to the level of peak performance.

AÏM FOR LIFE MASTERY™

Communication with Others

Our performance is supported by our strength to take the required action, in essence getting the ball rolling as self-talk does for you. Once we get the ball rolling, then we have to influence our surroundings.

We don't live on an island like hermits. People are around us, at home, at work, in social events, in leisure time, in pretty well everything we're involved with.

If self-talk is the foundation of our peak performance and ensures our success, the continuation of the process – our communication with others - is just as important, if not more so.

We cannot accomplish much without other people's help or cooperation.

If we're to remove barriers to our performance by our communication with others, I would suggest that a particular focus be directed to the intent of our communications.

Let me share a vivid example of how our communication to others can torpedo our effort.

Years ago while I was working with Larry Ring, then head coach of the University of Ottawa Gee-gees, I used to remind Larry of the impact of his discourse on the players. "Talk about what you want; don't talk about what you don't want!" used to be the refrain. One fine Saturday, we were playing Montreal's McGill University. There was about one minute left in the game, and we were losing by less than a touchdown. We got to their 3-yard line. The tension was palpable. Everyone was on edge. We had to make it to the end zone.

AÏM FOR LIFE MASTERY™

The offensive coordinator signalled the play in, but the quarterback could not get it, or didn't understand it. So he went into the huddle and called the only play he could think of under stress, the one that Larry had told him so many times not to run in such a situation. "Whatever you do, inside the 5-yard line, don't run the bootleg!" You see, Steve was a great quarterback but not fleet of foot. And as Larry had feared, Steve was stopped. By repeatedly telling Steve not to run the bootleg, he had programmed him to do so in a stressful situation. Luckily, the story has a positive end as we had another shot at scoring. This time it was successful, and we won the game.

This story reminds us that peak performance is also being aware of how we talk to others. Always be mindful of your purpose when you are talking; you never know when you could be working against yourself without realizing it.

We should always keep in mind and be aware of a few communication principles that are constantly at work. Once you start paying attention to the fact that you are always communicating, you will increase your awareness of the different mechanisms at work. You will recognize that listening is more powerful than talking; that the best results are produced when you make a 100% effort to understand the other person; and that when you strive to ensure that your perception is equal to the speaker's intention, you will have peak performance communication.

This is hard work; be mindful of that.

You've learned to communicate over your lifetime, but it may have been through less than effective techniques. After all, communications is not a subject of study in most curricula. It's considered a specialty - witness the college and university degrees in communication. The fact is that if you studied some other subject, not much fuss was made over communications,

AÏM FOR LIFE MASTERY™

and least of all, not about the key elements of effective communication.

To integrate peak performance, you will want to become more aware of the impact of communications on your results. Be conscious of how you talk to others and what is going on in your head with self-talk. With a little introspection, you will soon realize that your communications to yourself and to others have a large impact on how you will act. Just that awareness is guaranteed to boost your performance like you never thought possible.

AÏM FOR LIFE MASTERY™

Mastering Emotions

This subject is so vast that it would take a whole library to address all the aspects involved.

The following does not aim at a complete review but rather is an attempt at simplifying the approach to enable you to reach peak performance.

Many researchers have studied the subject, identified the framework, offered explanations, and suggested ways and means to corral our emotional nature as human beings.

I read Daniel Goleman[25] and his treatise on EQ (Emotional Quotient); studied the work of Albert Ellis[26] on rational emotive behaviour therapy; sought to understand the microbiology of feelings as Deepak Chopra[27] explains; read the work of Bandler and Grinder[28] on Neuro Linguistic Programming (NLP); read with great interest many other insights and techniques to modify emotions; and have lately come across the work of Lee Pulos[29] on the biology of empowerment.

What I've learned is based on knowledge of brain functions and the actual results I've obtained in applying the techniques in this book. It's based on Albert Ellis' work, and supported by NLP concepts and the theory of mental programming. A graphical description is included in Appendix 8, The ABC of Emotional Mastery.

---

[25] Goleman, Daniel. *Emotional Intelligence*. Bantam Books, 10th Anniversary Edition. New York 2006

[26] Ellis, Albert, Ph.D. and Lange, Arthur, Ph.D. *How to Keep People from Pushing Your Buttons*. Citadel. 2003

[27] Chopra, Deepak. *Ageless Body, Timeless Mind: The Quantum Alternative to Growing Old*. Three Rivers Press. 1994

[28] Bandler, Richard W. and Grinder, John T. *Frogs into Princes*. Real People Press. 1989

[29] Pulos, Dr. Lee. *The Biology of Empowerment*. CD audio program from Nightingale-Conant, 2009

AÏM FOR LIFE MASTERY™

In these modern times, we have a tendency to seek complicated answers. After all, we've uncovered so much information on just about everything. In the case of the human body, we are seeing further advances in technology which allow us to measure what is going on inside this wonderful machine. All these states that result from some imbalance in the body chemistry can be loosely coined as a "**dis-ease**".

The fact is that cause and effect are still the ruling factor. When it comes to emotions, we would do well to understand that they are the physical result of the secretion of hormones in our blood stream. What's important is to realize that the secretion of hormones causing emotions results from an action, a thinking action taking place in your brain.

In the context of this book, "dis-ease" is used to signify the lack of ease you may feel, whether physical, emotional or mental.

To better understand, let's think of breathing, blood circulation, digestion, healing, growing hair, reflex action, pain, cold and hot, all automatic responses to a central control system commonly known as the autonomous brain. It's a wonderful machine, always at work, keeping our metabolic functions in action, monitoring our chemical equilibrium to ensure stable conditions, keeping away "**dis-ease**" caused by imbalance, fighting invaders through our immune system. And all that activity happens without even one wilful conscious action from us.

Isn't that wonderful? Have you ever stopped to think about all that happens inside you, and you don't even have a clue how your body does it?

The real discovery is when we start reading about psychosomatic illnesses.

AÏM FOR LIFE MASTERY™

One common illness is stomach ulcers. They don't just happen. They are the result of our anxiety, our worry, and our fears. The stomach liner is one of the most dynamic parts of our body; it is renewed every thirty hours. The high acid content needed to digest our food would attack the best materials we can find. So our stomach must be protected –the cell rejuvenation process acts to rebuild our stomach lining.

If we interfere with that process, it makes for a weakened liner or stomach wall, and in the extreme, it will lose its ability to withstand the high acid content. One way we can interfere is by what we eat or drink. Too much alcohol for instance can result in an ulcer. But the rebuilding mechanism is controlled by the brain. If we hinder the normal function of that command system by our thinking, we can develop a weakness in the rebuilding process that results in an ulcer. We generate **dis-ease** in our own body.

The impact of our thinking on our brain functions can be understood by thinking of our reaction in certain circumstances.

Let's say you are driving on the road, and someone cuts you off, almost running you into the ditch. Close call! You have a surge of adrenaline that causes you to have certain emotions.

You might have fear first, then anger, then you cool down because after all, it's not worth it. All the feelings that occurred were the result of hormone secretion driven by your brain. You saw the car, you interpreted the potential outcome, you generated fear, then it turned to anger since you felt that the driver was stupid, and finally, the hormones subsided as you realized that it was better to ignore such a bad driver.

All that happened automatically, more or less, guided by your mental models which gave value and meaning to the events. The meaning was translated into a thought that generated the hormone secretion, and resulted in the sequence of feelings (commonly known as emotions). The action of thinking in your brain generated the secretion of the unwanted hormones.

You're probably wondering what this has to do with peak performance. I know that your beliefs might make it hard for you to agree with this explanation, but I would just encourage you to stop and think of your own experiences. Be honest with yourself.

Contrary to conventional thinking, feelings do follow action, the action of your brain capturing the stimulus (being cut off on the road), assessing and evaluating against your deep down beliefs (careless driving can kill), attributing a value to the action (it's bad), and causing your brain to launch the reaction system – secretion of emotion-causing hormones leading to the feelings experienced throughout the event. And it all happened like magic. Well, that's what happens in any situation. We are feeling beings, and we give meaning to events or stimuli. Thus, we can cause "**dis-ease**" like ulcers in our body.

Here comes peak performance. If we can create such a reaction inside our body, maybe we should think of the opposite, how we can affect how we feel, which emotion to generate in order to aim for peak performance?

The example of the stomach ulcer can be used to support the view that we can indeed **master** our emotions. Just look around, and notice some people are calm, others are nervous, some are reactive, and others are deliberate. It all has to do with emotional mastery, the ability to harness our thought processes and make them do what we want in certain circumstances.

It's not easy.

Like anything else, the first step is to be aware of what's going on inside yourself, how you view and interpret stimuli (activating events).

AÏM FOR LIFE MASTERY™

Once you've taken the time to realize that you can transform the way you see things, that you can produce different results, then you can choose to act differently. The next step is to develop a tool or method to deal with those times when you find yourself reacting in disagreement with the way you desire.

> *You have a life of thinking habits to unlearn and relearn. Remember to use the power of words for your benefit. Change your usual tendency to be "impatient" to "I'm patient".*

As I keep telling my clients who sometimes get impatient with the slowness of results, "The trick is to modify your thinking around the word ***impatient***. Insert an apostrophe and a space and you have your patience-building mantra: ***I'm patient***".

Don't kid yourself; you have years of established behaviours or habits to overcome. The good thing is that research has demonstrated beyond doubt that we can develop new thinking pathways (reprogram our brain) in 20-30 days. Patience and perseverance will be your friends in getting it done. Persistent action will bring the rewards you seek.

So pick up your courage, dedicate yourself to transforming your emotional outcome, and reap the benefits! You will gain so much by developing **emotional mastery**. One thing for sure, you'll learn to be more flexible, and enjoy the ability to choose your reaction more easily when faced with unexpected events. That's when you will become a peak performer.

As the Chinese proverb says, "Anger closes our eyes and opens our mouth." Anger stands for any emotion that tends to blur our vision and reduces our ability to think straight.

If we accept the premise that peak performance is **the right stuff, in the right amount, at the right time**™, it is obvious that we will want to remove barriers to peak performance by gaining emotional mastery.

AÏM FOR LIFE MASTERY™

Just think how much more powerful and capable you can become when you can decide how you will react to certain events. Choose to be "reasonably" upset as opposed to being "overly" upset because your emotions got the best of you. In the long run, you will reduce your stress and gain enjoyment of life.

Making Decisions

Another barrier to peak performance presents itself almost daily. It's the seeming inability to make the right decision, the right choice in line with your goals.

I bring this up because it's a common challenge that most of my clients face. When you decide to turn on the peak performance tap, you're going squarely against a lifetime of experiences where you have dilly-dallied and lost an opportunity. The barrier that kept you from creating the best result was a lack of focus on using the right process to make the right choice.

Let me explain "the right choice".

Some people will argue it's impossible to make "the right choice". How do you know the future? How can you account for the unexpected? How will you deal with issues where you clearly don't have the tools to be effective? And the questioning goes on until you back off.

For me, the right choice is located at the same place as all other critical or important aspects of your life. It's what you want to make it (design might be a better word, in line with your life vision or goal).

It is indeed impossible, or nearly so, to make the "right choice" when we don't have a clear view of the future.

The unknown is a monster that we seldom tame in the absence of a clear vision. So what is a person to do to arrive at "the right decision"? Again, let's keep it super simple. And let's go back to basics. Decision-making is a process that can be made effective and efficient if we take a serious look at minimizing waste.

But we must be clear on one fact; decision-making will suffer if there isn't a well-defined aim or goal. Just like there is a process to make sure of hitting a Bull's-eye on a practice target, decision-making can be made a lot easier by using a well-oiled process.

Such a process was developed by Kepner and Tregoe[30] in the mid-sixties. It is based on a determination of the factors that will ensure you hit your target (decision). A sample template is included in Appendix 9 (Decision Analysis Template) to illustrate how you can simplify the decision-making process to increase the chances of hitting the Bull's-eye with your decision. The objective or goal sought in a decision should be aligned to the vision of your future. If you have a clear vision of your future (what you want your life to be), it will become easier to identify the details associated with the decision (criteria or factors).

Once criteria are identified, they should be prioritized according to four levels of importance – MUST (GO or NO GO), HIGH WANT, MEDIUM WANT and LOW WANT.

It takes effort to assign the level of importance. After all, we're used to viewing everything as important. But is that really true? Don't you think that criteria or reasons for making a decision have different weights?

Think for example, about buying a car.

Most people have had the experience of doing the thinking around that. What criteria would you use? I'm sure you realize already that your criteria will not be those of your neighbour. They will relate to your needs.

[30] Kepner, Charles and Dr Tregoe, Benjamin. Founders, The Kepner-Tregoe Rational Process.

156   **PP = the right stuff, in the right amount, at the right time™**

AÏM FOR LIFE MASTERY™

Therefore, an easier way to clarify your decision might be to ask, "Why do I need this? or "Should I get this feature?" or "What can I afford?" We can go all the way to, "What will the neighbour think?" even though I would recommend that this question be rated very low on the importance scale.

Accordingly, you will choose criteria that must be fulfilled as the starting point. The procedure recommends a maximum of two or three MUSTs. You want to have only a few that squarely establish whether an option should or should not be considered. In the case of buying a house for example, available down payment will be a MUST. For a young family, access to schools will potentially be another. A third might simply be the space required; a two bedroom will not accommodate a family of five, unless you want to use triple bunk beds. Make your MUSTs truly MUSTs. Then the rest of the criteria can be assigned high, medium or low value depending on what you really care to have in the option you choose.

I believe that "the right decision" is possible as long as you have a clear focus on the desired result, and you're ready to make tough choices on assigning value to the criteria you choose to use for the decision analysis.

The whole idea is to remove the emotions from the process so that you have a decision based on facts, and not on feelings or emotions. You are free to choose as always, but if you want to maximize your results and integrate peak performance in your daily life, learning to make "the right choice" is another tool that you will want to add to your arsenal.

Let's consider the following example. A number of years back, I decided to buy a new house. I wanted it to meet a number of requirements. I had my own business and a need for my daughter's space. However, there were a number of other factors to consider.

AÏM FOR LIFE MASTERY™

Among them, suburban living, spacious garage, significant lot with trees, distance to shopping, bus accessibility (daughter going to school in the city), close to main thoroughfare, close to park land, finished basement, less than 10 years old, entrance facing south, all within an affordable down payment and mortgage.

Obviously, only 2-3 of these could be MUSTs, otherwise I would have never found the place. I had to grade the order of importance – affordability, location and room were my MUSTs. The rest were of a varying degree of WANT. Using the template, I selected from amongst the choices offered by the real estate agent.

The exercise turned out to be rather easy as I had preset the weight of each factor. I was able to quickly compare the common features and select three houses. The final choice came down to a score for each house, with the one selected having the highest score.

I still live in that house and congratulate myself almost every day for using a decision-making process that gave me a real winner.

AÏM FOR LIFE MASTERY™

Measuring Progress

A few years back, I read a book entitled *Getting Results* by Michael Leboeuf, Ph.D. His research had led him to write about what moves people to repeat behaviour. The concept is simple: what gets rewarded gets done.

Another key indicator came from Nelson Riis, a friend who read the draft of my book, and was kind enough to remind me of the importance of measuring progress. Since personal transformation is a stepwise process, it would be helpful to guide the reader through a system by which there is confirmation that indeed, this process works.

In all that you've read through this book, these next thoughts may be the most important to ensure your success toward peak performance. Indeed, we often decide on goals, how we will reach them, and get on with the work required until it's done. The problem is that too seldom do we stop along the way to assess how we're doing. Two things happen. The first is that we don't get the satisfaction of the last step we took. We omit celebration of success; we omit rewarding ourselves. We stay focused on the end result and forget to recognize the progress we've made. The second is that we often miss the opportunity to learn from having taken the last step, an opportunity to get better!

Throughout this process of integrating peak performance, I encourage you to become aware of the value that you will gain from taking stock of your progress as you practice the various steps of programming. If you put a focus on the task, and raise your awareness of what is happening inside you, you will facilitate

---

AÏM FOR LIFE MASTERY™

the growth of your mastery of anything you're working on. Measuring how you're doing will be key to providing the useful feedback that feeds your motivation.

In my 20 years plus of coaching people in peak performance, I've observed that those who take time to reflect on their progress do much better. For one, the old adage that "feedback is the breakfast of champions" applies in spades. How can one improve or move on to higher levels without feedback that provides a sense of progress? The other thing is, that the more you reflect on what's happening inside you as you program yourself for peak performance, the more you will gain awareness and get in touch with that part of you that drives to success.

I want to make this measurement as simple as possible. I would suggest that you establish a notebook for recording your performance. After each session, take time to reflect and jot down the results of your training. Make sure to record the date, the mental exercises you did, and the benefit you sense at the end. It will take a little while to get accustomed to the process. With time, it will become a step of your journey that you'll enjoy because you'll soon start to notice that "what gets rewarded gets done". Putting focus on measuring your journey will bring the satisfaction and the belief that you're moving in the right direction.

I've mentioned reflection. The key is to step back after each mental gym session and check how you feel about the new ability you are developing. If it's a physical performance, review the result of your last outing. For instance, if we look at sports, golf would be a good one. Are you more relaxed? Do you still tense up when you see water ahead of you? How is the little voice talking? Do you have a "can do" feeling, or one of "oh no, not again"?

If you look at a business situation, check to see if you're still stressed by the presence of a certain person.

AÏM FOR LIFE MASTERY™

Do you feel overwhelmed by the task at hand? Do you feel like running away, or can you take the challenge head on? Those are all indicators of the transformation that is going on in your subconscious brain. The mental models of the past are being replaced by the new way of thinking produced by your relaxation, affirmation, visualization, and gratitude processes.

The fact is that the more you reflect and record your reflections, the more you'll be able to connect; and the more you connect with your subconscious self, the more you'll be able to mould it to serve you in the best and worst of times. Measuring your progress will enable you to get the results you are seeking. Failing to do that will slow down your progress, and perhaps might even stop it. "What gets measured gets done".

Making sure that you assess your progress will strengthen your motivation to move ahead and tackle whatever obstacle happens on your journey to **peak performance**. It's not rocket science. Just think about your everyday life. When you gain happiness because you've accomplished something, you usually get a renewed sense of energy. You feel empowered and ready to take on a bigger challenge. It's the way our brain works.

Therefore, in order to remove further barriers from your path to peak performance, make sure you measure your progress. Be aware of the changes that are happening, as little as they may be. They're the little victories over your past mental models, the ones that didn't bring the desired results. Congratulate yourself, and congratulate your subconscious brain for moving in the direction of effort-less effectiveness. The more you become conscious of your progress, the more you will release the power you have to make things happen. Remember the neural networks. Once your brain gets wired for peak performance in one area of your daily life, it will expand that capability into other areas of your life.

AÏM FOR LIFE MASTERY™

Some might say "it's magic". The fact is we all have that capability to decide and transform our thinking into a way that makes it easier to accomplish with less effort. The end result is increased performance while reducing stress, which is the ultimate goal of peak performance for any human being.

Key Points to Remember

There are a few factors in your life that can impede your progress in developing the ability to create peak performance. If you are to minimize the effort and install a process that is more in line with effort-less effectiveness, you will do well to familiarize yourself with the following:

- Paradigm shifts: we all operate with mental models (thinking pathways) that allow us to be on "automatic" and reduce the effort to get things done. However, some of these mental models or pathways have a tendency to slow us down as opposed to liberate our natural capabilities. Remember the 7 paradigm shifts that can make or break your journey to peak performance: 1) rigid to flexible; 2) necessity to possibility; 3) blaming to helping; 4) judging to evaluating; 5) complaining to problem-solving; 6) scattered to focused; 7) liking to loving.

- Communications barriers: beware and stay aware of the impact of your communications to yourself and to others. The words you use can torpedo your effort or make it easier to reach your intended goals. The choice is yours.

- Mastering emotions: it is now proven that Emotional Quotient (EQ) is more important than Intelligence Quotient (IQ). When you learn to master your emotions, you tremendously increase your capability to seek peak performance. Remember the A-B-C of Rational Emotive Behaviour Therapy. Use the thinking wedge to create space between stimulus and your response. See the vision of your future clearly.

AÏM FOR LIFE MASTERY™

- Making decisions: in your journey to peak performance, you will greatly benefit from being decisive. Learning a method to become objective about making decisions will reduce doubts and hesitation in advancing toward your goals. A systematic and structured approach will make decision-making a relative breeze and help you make the "right choice".

- Measuring progress: progress is facilitated by measurement. It is the activity that provides feedback on how well you are doing on your journey to mastery. It is suggested that you get serious about a measurement system that will track how well you are achieving the pre-set goals on your journey to excellence.

CONCLUSION AND PATH
FORWARD

You have travelled the path to learn how to set **peak performance** as a habit in your life.

In this book, we emphasized the need to develop a clear direction for your efforts. We also reviewed how you can minimize deviations from that set direction through a sense of mission (why) and a set of values (guardrails) that will keep you on your chosen path.

We've learned about the impact of **relaxing your body** to slow down your mental processes and thus create clear thinking. Through NLP techniques, we've put in place ways and means (affirmations and visualization) to anchor *new mental models* (thinking pathways) that will serve as **automatics** to create **mastery** in your everyday life. To make sure that your emotional being follows you on the journey, we've assigned a great value to **gratitude** and the technique to chase away **fear**.

All these actions will be less than effective unless you remember to go to your mental gym every day and practice these concepts!

Remember, the brain is like a garden. If you don't feed it and cultivate it, it will grow weeds.

Weeds are not desirable if you want to attain and maintain peak performance in your everyday life.

The right stuff, in the right amount, at the right time™ is an undeniable fact. We must strive to eliminate waste and make best

AÏM FOR LIFE MASTERY™

use of our resources of time, energy, and abilities. Otherwise, we may fall short on our desired results and live to say "If only I'd ….".

The choice is yours. It's your life. One thing is for sure. You won't be able to ignore this new knowledge. Having gained awareness of what is going on inside you, you won't be able to look at life the way you did before. You are now on a journey to increase your results while reducing your stress.

It is said that knowledge is power. More appropriately, it might be better to say "the proper use of knowledge creates power". You can now see that without action, a vision is just a dream. And as Joel Barker[31] points out, action without vision just passes the time. Only when action is coupled to a vision can we transform the world (starting with oneself).

The key to your future success depends on having a clear vision of your future. Remember Einstein's quote: "The best way to have a bright future is to create it." It doesn't matter if your direction requires adjustment along the way. The key is to have something to aim at. Only when you have a clear aim can you apply the full force of your desire to reach your goal. Otherwise, you're on an uncertain voyage leading to God knows where.

To be a peak performer, a clear vision of the future is critical in aligning your knowledge, abilities, skills and expertise to progress effectively, and avoid costly curves. Alignment on purpose leads to "effort-less effectiveness", the state of **peak performance**.

A Simple Recipe

We've travelled through the elements of the **AïM Program**™, emphasizing the need for awareness, the first step to peak performance. We've also seen that unless you internalize the

---

[31] Barker, Joel. *Discovering the Future Series: The Power of Vision.* Video program. Star Thrower Distribution, Inc. 1991

concept or idea that you recognized as mission critical, you will not be consistent in the application of peak performance.

But beyond including the idea or concept in your bag of tricks, you must teach yourself to integrate the idea into your daily routine, make it part of the skills, abilities, knowledge and expertise that support your efforts.

And finally, in order to ensure that you will be adept at using the technique or process of peak performance, you must practice consistently, all the time, just like your physical muscles. Without practice, muscles lose their tone and strength. The same applies for mental abilities.

In order to have peak performance - **the right stuff, in the right amount, at the right** © - the recipe must be uniform, consistent, and applied in a repeatable and reliable way. It is the basis of quality management and continuous improvement, and it applies at all levels of performance. The **AïM Program**™ provides that process and guides you on a journey to excellence. How far you go is totally up to you.

Success ONLY After Hard Work

It is a law of nature that cannot be denied - "To every action, there is an opposite and equal reaction." In technical terms,

> The reality is that "success" comes before "work" only in the dictionary.

energy cannot be destroyed, only transformed from one state to another. In order to create success in what you do, you have to work at transforming the gifts you have accumulated over your lifetime into tools that produce peak performance at every opportunity.

Ask any outstanding business person or top athlete; they will tell you how hard they worked to get to where they are now. Success can only be achieved through hard work. In peak performance

AÏM FOR LIFE MASTERY™

the same law applies. Perhaps it's not hard work in the sense of physical effort. In peak performance, the term "hard work" applies, and refers to focused and sustained mental rehearsal to ensure that your automatic response under fire will be aligned to your desired outcomes.

One way to ensure that you will always include your mental gym (hard work) in your life is to make it part of your daily agenda. Plan 15 minutes, morning and at night time before going to bed. Make sure it is clearly marked on your calendar or in your agenda book, or if you're technically minded, put an alarm in your cell phone! Just like you need air to live, your mental gym is your passport to peak performance.

You will want to take time to relax, affirm, visualize, express gratitude and reinforce your trigger so that in times of need, when you feel unsure, or doubt your ability, you can trigger yourself into a performance state (the ZONE) on command. In that way, you will increase your potential for hitting the mark and in so doing, increase the W.I.N. You will gain the ability to take care of "what's important now!"

Be sure to develop a deep down belief that your key to success in creating peak performance on a consistent basis is to practice, practice, practice (hard work) in a uniform, consistent, and repeatable way.

Help Is Always There

You have invested much time in becoming more aware of what you need to develop peak performance in your life. As I mentioned at the beginning, was there much discovery in your reading? Or do you agree that there was "nothing new" here? Do you find that you have now raised your awareness about ideas and concepts that are part of your everyday life? Isn't it true that this exercise reminded you of many facts you've known all along?

AÏM FOR LIFE MASTERY™

What you now have is a structured and systematic process to ensure that you integrate the knowledge, skills and abilities you've built over a lifetime into most of the challenges you will face. However, if you still feel a need to further clarify or define the concepts or ideas you've reviewed, I'd be pleased to answer questions, bring clarification, and even accept your suggestions in order to deepen your understanding of the concepts and the process of **the right stuff, in the right amount, at the right time**™ and make it work even better for you.

To reach me, you can either write or send an email and I'll be happy to provide further explanations and coaching in the application of the **AïM Program**™. My goal here is to share with you a proven process that can make a world of difference for you in all aspects of your life. It's a process by which you can transform your results from an acceptable level to an outstanding level whenever you choose to aim for that goal.

I encourage you to become proactive and forward looking in deciding to apply **the right stuff, in the right amount, at the right time**™. Your life will become a personal journey to excellence and peak performance.

AÏM FOR LIFE MASTERY™
APPENDICES

APPENDICES

1. Building a Compelling Vision of Your Future

2. A List of Values

3. The 3R Process©

4. Brain Wave Patterns

5. Developing Powerful Affirmations

6. Visualizing for Effective Reprogramming

7. Secrets of Peak Performance in Communications

8. The A-B-C of Emotional Mastery

9. Decision Analysis Template

10. Life Successes Inventory

APPENDIX 1

Building a compelling vision of your future

This is a process by which you can design the image or portrait (vision) of what you want to achieve in the future. The look ahead is usually around 10 years. The time interval makes it within the realm of possibility, but not so close that you tend to restrict the view with barriers that might exist today. The main reason for the look ahead is to create a picture of a desired future on which you want your subconscious brain to lock on. It creates a desired state from where it is possible to look back, and define what actions will take you there.

Your subconscious brain will act as a homing device to guide you in moments when you may stray from the straight line that takes you to the vision of your future.

Joel Baker, a futurist, identified three characteristics that should be reflected in your vision statement. You will want your vision to be:

- **Positive and inspiring** (our subconscious brain doesn't know the difference between what is imagined and what is real; make it powerful and heart grabbing, so that it moves you whenever you read it).
- **Shared and supported** (since we're not alone in the world, you'll want to involve a loved one or close friends in looking to the future with enthusiasm).
- **Detailed and comprehensive** (the more details you'll include, the more you'll engage your senses (emotions) in driving you forward to the vision).

AÏM FOR LIFE MASTERY™
APPENDICES

Furthermore, as we are total human beings, your vision should touch on all aspects of life. Experts such as Lee Pulos and Joel Barker recommend that your vision touch upon a spectrum of domains that compose your total life:

- Physical – health, fitness, strength, capability
- Mental – mastery of thinking, ability to think clearly, being calm and focused
- Emotional – develop emotional intelligence to be able to choose how you will react to situations
- Psychological – well-adjusted, free of misconceptions, ability to be rational when required
- Spiritual – knowing your place in the universe, understanding your life purpose
- Financial – monetary status, assets
- Professional – who you are and what that allows you to do in life, personal growth
- Social – your involvement in society, giving of time and knowledge
- Family – relationships with loved ones, personal situation (married, kids, etc.)
- Leisure – hobbies, main interests, travel, sports, friends
- Philanthropy – supporting intrinsic human need to give
- Any other that you would choose to define where you want to be in 10 years

The vision statement should respect the 3P Rule – it should be Personal (I am, I do, I live...); Present (as if already happened); Positive (liberate the subconscious brain to act).

AÏM FOR LIFE MASTERY™
APPENDICES

The vision statement should build an image of the future that you want to make happen in your life.

A Word of Caution
Make sure you focus on the image of your desired future when you put the words together. Use descriptive words, and avoid stating the reasons why or the actions you will take to get there. That's called "a mission statement". The following is a quote from the Nightingale-Conant website which characterizes what a mission statement is:

Mission Statement:
A purposeful promise that carries you toward your goals.

A well thought out, goal-focused (aimed at a clear vision of the future) mission statement can act as an achievement coach — giving you the focus, direction, and accountability you need to accomplish your career, financial, and personal goals (vision).

An Example of a Compelling Vision

The following is an actual vision statement written by one of my young clients, age 16, whom I guided through the exercise. It combines both the vision and mission statements for that individual. Reference to actual names or places have been removed to protect identity.

Please note that the vision and mission statements are combined. This statement covers many aspects of a person's life as discussed previously. The reasons that are included refer to why (mission) the vision is attractive and will act as a PULL.

His Vision Statement (unedited) 10 years in the future

I am 26 years old and a successful person academically, with my own career, friendships and relationships. I am very strong mentally, physically, and emotionally when dealing with difficult and challenging situations. When talking about success academically, I refer to the university degree, and the Master's degree I've obtained from an academically focused and strong university. This allows me to foresee an occupation that I enjoy and have fun doing each day after my basketball career, essentially to live a happier life. I am an electrical engineer, and consider this is the profession I want to exercise in the future. This prospect allows me to live without having to deal with difficult financial situations because it produces a fulfilling pay check that I can invest into different banking options and accounts to save for the future.

Presently, that is my backup life plan while I am working on my basketball career. My potential has taken me to Europe to play in a professional league, with an ultimate dream of the NBA. During my university life, I attended a school in the United States which had a strong academic program as well as a competitive basketball program that competed with the top schools in the NCAA. I worked towards this everyday by practicing basketball, working extremely hard in school, and learning the whole mental aspect of basketball in life by working with a performance coach and applying the different types of exercises that built my mind mastery.

I am heavily active and involved with my family by taking care of everyone and keeping close bonds by getting together for family reunions for different occasions such as Christmas or Thanksgiving. Moreover, by being a generous, trustworthy and kind person, I look to build friendly relationships with new people and maintain the close ties with my current friends because I understand how important it is to have a strong social life in terms of helping to ensure that you can experience more joy within your life.

In terms of spirituality, I picture myself as somebody who understands his place in the world by working hard to accomplish my goals, and to help other people around me by having the significant values such as having integrity, being generous and giving, being respectful, working with others efficiently to ensure that everyone can achieve the optimal level of happiness, and just being someone who people can look up to and see a strong human being with the ability to always make the right decisions, even in difficult times, and to help people when they are in need and to be empathetic towards them.

I ensure that I give back to my community which helped make me the person I am today. I help the people that are in need but aren't able to help themselves effectively. I credit much of my development to the xxxxxx region who through the different basketball associations that I played with helped me become more social by putting me in situations with new and different people every day, enabling me to become sociable. I help coach a team, or work with the programs by donating money or in some other form. Furthermore, I look to help the people and kids of xxxxxxxx. I help provide opportunities for the many young children that have the potential to live successful lives, but aren't awarded the opportunities because of a lack of money or family support. I help to set up different tutoring programs by donating my time to help different kids and to provide assistance to their different educational and recreational activities in any way possible.

I see myself as a successful human being, who is healthy, well-liked for my strong values and traits and someone who has accomplished many different things such as earning a university degree, and leading a fulfilling career in basketball. I look forward to being a professional engineer after my basketball career is over.

<u>A Guiding Light Toward His Future</u>
As you can see, he was very detailed in describing who and what he wants to be ten years down the road. This statement will act as a PULL in helping him make good choices for his life. He'll likely hit the mark. And if things change, it will be easier for him to adjust since he is aiming at something that is compelling and inspiring.

APPENDIX 2

A List of Values

The following is a list of values that have been identified through a thorough review of human characteristics in the workplace or in community activities. They were compiled by Bill Belanger, a retired emeritus professor at the University of Ottawa, Ontario, Canada.

They are provided as a reminder of the multiple values that are at work in every situation we encounter in our everyday life. When considering the root of a person's behaviour or response under a particular circumstance, it's useful to remember that we're all different. Thus, it becomes more acceptable to think in terms of "different" as opposed to "wrong" when evaluating or judging another person's thinking.

The list also provides a reference for establishing accurately the few values that you choose to act as your guardrails on your journey to peak performance.

List of Recognized Values

In the following list, you will no doubt recognize many of the values you identify with. Some may also be foreign to you. This list was composed over time and should be reviewed with curiosity and a sense of discovery.

To each his own. The important thing is to become more aware of what makes you act in a certain way under certain circumstances, and you don't even think how it happens.

It just happens!

AÏM FOR LIFE MASTERY™
APPENDICES

1. Accountability
2. Activity
3. Admiration
4. Adventure
5. Affirmation
6. Authenticity
7. Autonomy
8. Blamelessness
9. Caring
10. Caution
11. Character
12. Charity
13. Collaboration
14. Comfort
15. Commitment
16. Communication
17. Competence
18. Competitiveness
19. Compliance
20. Confidence
21. Congruence
22. Consensus
23. Consideration
24. Consistency
25. Contentment
26. Contribution
27. Cooperation
28. Courage
29. Courtesy
30. Creativity
31. Credibility
32. Decency
33. Deference
34. Democracy
35. Dependability
36. Discipline
37. Discretion
38. Distinction
39. Emotion
40. Encouragement
41. Equitability
42. Self-esteem
43. Fairness
44. Faithfulness
45. Fidelity
46. Flexibility
47. Forgiveness
48. Freedom
49. Friendliness
50. Frugality
51. Gentleness
52. Genuineness
53. Happiness
54. Hard work
55. Harmony
56. Honesty
57. Honour
58. Hope
59. Humour
60. Independence
61. Individuality
62. Industry
63. Innovation
64. Inspiration
65. Integrity
66. Interdependence
67. Involvement
68. Joy
69. Justice
70. Kindness
71. Legitimacy
72. Loyalty
73. Love
74. Mannerliness
75. Materialism
76. Meekness
77. Mercy
78. Merit

PP = the right stuff, in the right amount, at the right time™

79.	Moderation	115.	Respectability
80.	Morality	116.	Respect
81.	Motherhood	117.	Respectfulness
82.	Neatness	118.	Responsibility
83.	Nobleness	119.	Romanticism
84.	Obedience	120.	Self-discipline
85.	Openness	121.	Sensitivity
86.	Opportunity	122.	Sincerity
87.	Optimism	123.	Skillfulness
88.	Orderly	124.	Spirituality
89.	Originality	125.	Spontaneity
90.	Patience	126.	Stability
91.	Patriotism	127.	Status
92.	Peacefulness	128.	Stinginess
93.	Personable	129.	Tactfulness
94.	Piety	130.	Teamwork
95.	Playfulness	131.	Temperance
96.	Pleasantness	132.	Tenacity
97.	Poise	133.	Thoughtfulness
98.	Politeness	134.	Thrift
99.	Popularity	135.	Tolerance
100.	Positivity	136.	Tranquility
101.	Possessiveness	137.	Trust
102.	Potential	138.	Trustworthiness
103.	Power	139.	Truth
104.	Practicality	140.	Truthfulness
105.	Pragmatism	141.	Uniqueness
106.	Productivity	142.	Uprightness
107.	Prudence	143.	Validity
108.	Punctuality	144.	Veracity
109.	Quietness	145.	Virtuosity
110.	Rationality	146.	Virtuousness
111.	Recognition	147.	Wisdom
112.	Reliability		
113.	Reputation		
114.	Resourcefulness		

AÏM FOR LIFE MASTERY™
APPENDICES

APPENDIX 3

The 3R Process©

The **3R Process**© (REST/RELAX/RECHARGE) was designed as a method to produce rest, relaxation and the recharging of your emotional batteries. It is based on: 1) the use of programmed breathing; 2) the ability of the brain to be programmed to act in an unconscious way; and 3) repetition to anchor the process. Applying the technique as described integrates the ability to rest at will, to get rid of stress on command, and to regenerate your emotional energy at any time, any place, or in any situation.

The process is simple and should be practiced in a rigorous and consistent manner, always repeating the same action to anchor the concept. Doing the exercise for at least twenty-one days (twice per day) ensures that the pattern is imprinted on the brain. The new **3R Habit**© can then be recalled simply by taking the **3R Posture**©. The sitting posture (as opposed to lying down) allows anchoring of a process that can be used in any circumstance. It is recommended that the **3R Process**© be practiced first thing in the morning, and before bedtime.

Programming the 3R Process©

The **3R POSTURE**© requires that you sit motionless in a straight chair, shoulders back, chin up, hands resting on your knees - palms up, feet flat on the floor. It should be done in a quiet and comfortable place.

Breathe in through the nose (**I**), hold your breath (**H**), and exhale through your mouth (**E**) in a controlled fashion. The 3-step (**IHE**) programmed breathing should be done (ideally) in a proportion of 1-4-2 (or ex., **INHALE** -3 seconds, **HOLD** -12 seconds, **EXHALE** -6 seconds). Expand the abdomen (rather than the chest) while breathing in to: 1) optimize the use of the total lung capacity; and 2) get maximum oxygen intake. If you have trouble doing 1-4-2, you should at least make the ratios 1-1-1.

Repeat for 5-7 minutes while remaining motionless and blanking your mind. Saying the word "STOP" or seeing it in your mind (visualizing), will help to stop the spinning in your brain (mental activity).

AÏM FOR LIFE MASTERY™
APPENDICES

To develop an automatic subconscious **3R Response**© to the posture, use the table and repeat for twenty-one days morning and night, checking a box each time you do the exercise. Like going to the gym to develop your muscles, the brain training strengthens your mental capability. Make this practice part of your daily routine.

Repeating the exercise will create new thinking pathways in your subconscious brain which will allow you to eliminate stress and initiate relaxation on command.

3R Process© Programming Table (enter days of the month)

DAY	1	2	3	4	5	6	7
Date							
a.m.							
p.m.							
DAY	8	9	10	11	12	13	14
Date							
a.m.							
p.m.							
DAY	15	16	17	18	19	20	21
Date							
a.m.							
p.m.							

© Copyright, Raymond Perras 1993-2011
PEAK PERFORMANCE TECHNIQUES©

APPENDIX 4

Brain Wave patterns

The following is a short summary excerpt drawn from Wikipedia. It describes the common brain waves observed in the human brain. It is provided to situate the "alpha waves" which is the level of brain activity we seek in the programmed breathing exercise. The alpha wave level allows consciousness while reducing the subconscious brain's resistance to suggestions created by affirmations and visualization.

Reaching the alpha state through relaxation breathing sets the stage for installing new mental programs. It makes the reprogramming effort more effective and requires less time to produce results. Frequency of the wave patterns is called hertz (Hz), and is defined as number of cycles per second in a periodic phenomenon.

Delta waves
Delta is the frequency range up to 4 Hz. It tends to be the highest in amplitude and the slowest waves. It's normally seen in adults in slow wave sleep or deep sleep. It's also normally seen in babies. It's usually most prominent frontally in adults (e.g. FIRDA - Frontal Intermittent Rhythmic Delta).

Theta waves
Theta is the frequency range from 4 Hz to 8 Hz. Theta is seen normally in young children. It may be seen in drowsiness or arousal in older children and adults; it can also be seen in meditation. This range has been associated with reports of relaxed, meditative, creative and sleeping states

Alpha waves.
Alpha is the frequency range from 8 Hz to 13 Hz. Hans Berger named the first rhythmic EEG activity he saw as the "alpha wave". This was

the "posterior basic rhythm" (also called the "posterior dominant rhythm" or the "posterior alpha rhythm"), seen in the posterior regions of the head on both sides, higher in amplitude on the dominant side. It emerges with closing of the eyes and with relaxation, and attenuates with eye opening or mental exertion. It is a <u>most suggestible state</u>.

Beta waves.
Beta is the frequency range from 14 Hz to about 30 Hz. It's usually seen on both sides in symmetrical distribution, and is most evident frontally. Beta activity is closely linked to motor behavior and is generally attenuated during active movements. Low amplitude beta with multiple and varying frequencies is often associated with active, busy or anxious thinking and active concentration. Rhythmic beta with a dominant set of frequencies is associated with various pathologies and drug effects, especially benzodiazepines. It may be absent or reduced in areas of cortical damage. It's the dominant rhythm in patients who are alert or anxious or who have their eyes open.

Gamma waves.
Gamma is the frequency range approximately 30–100 Hz (notionally around 40 Hz). Gamma rhythms are thought to represent binding of different populations of neurons together into a network for the purpose of carrying out a certain cognitive or motor function. The reader is encouraged to search for more explanations if a more detailed understanding is required.

APPENDIX 5

Developing Powerful Affirmations

One effective way to program our subconscious brain is to use self-talk, more commonly known as the little voice in your head.

It's at work all the time, and if unchecked, tends to drive your thinking process astray. Many of us have been programmed negatively since infanthood by well-meaning parents and other caregivers. Think of the many times when you were little, where you were told "No" over and over again. "Don't touch, you will hurt yourself". "You're too small". If you got too close to the edge of the water (pool or lake), you were admonished about the danger of falling into the water. If you tried to eat something that had fallen on the floor, you were told that was dirty, "Don't put that in your mouth".

The string of negative feedback was endless, albeit with the right intentions. No wonder that our subconscious brain was imprinted with a slant toward the negative as a first response. Now that you've reached adulthood, when faced with any stimulus or situation, you have a natural tendency to first see its negative side. Your subconscious brain generates questions that direct focus on "what could go wrong", "what if…", "will I be able…", all directed at doubt and uncertainty. Isn't it time to switch that little voice to one that directs your thinking toward the positive side of the equation?

There is good news. Just as you got programmed when you were younger, and you continue to be programmed by the advertisement industry, you can use the same approach to reprogram yourself. By using a uniform, consistent, and repeatable verbal message, you can create new synapses in your subconscious brain that affect your automatic thinking, and help you react to situations in a way that is most effective and productive for you.

The technique is called "affirmations". It consists of the repeated use of a statement that describes the state that you want to reach in your daily life. For example, if you are a smoker and want to quit, you can install a mental program using the words, "I am a non-smoker and I enjoy all the benefits of my smoke-free environment". You can increase the impact by adding something about the financial burden, the improved health aspect, and even the nice breath that you now enjoy.

Repeating the "affirmation" in a structured and systematic way will, over time, install a new belief in your subconscious brain that will make you move away from smoking with minimal effort. The key is to do the affirmation in an efficient and effective way that creates the new synapses in your brain.

Powerful Affirmations for Effective Mental Reprogramming

The recommended recipe is as follows:

1. Write your affirmation using the 3P Rule: make it personal (I am, I do, etc.), write it in the present (as if already happened) and make it positive (use words that avoid a negative statement like "I'm a non-smoker" as opposed to "I don't smoke"). Make sure you always have your affirmation available for consistent and uniform mental repetition.

2. When you do the affirmation, use a relaxation technique (like the 3R Process) to prepare the ground, put your subconscious brain into the alpha state. This will reduce the natural resistance of your subconscious brain to accept the new idea you're working to install.

3. Read your affirmation aloud 3-5 times. You will touch your subconscious brain through the optical nerve (read), the auditory nerve (hearing yourself) and the sensory feeling nerves of your cranial region (as your voice resonates). This provides a massive impact on your brain to anchor the message in many regions of your short term and long term memory. With repeated action, the synapses thus created (connections

between various regions of your brain) will become a new program that will help install a new way to interpret any stimulus related to the desired state.

4. Use no more than three affirmations at a time. You want your subconscious brain to focus on a minimum of ideas at one time. Too many affirmations will confuse your brain and reduce the impact. It will increase the time taken to make them permanent and likely may weaken your ability to adopt the new mental model you're trying to develop. Over time, you may develop the opinion that it's not working, and you will lose the benefit of the mental work you're doing.

5. Optimally, I recommend that you address three different areas of performance at once – focus on a physical, a mental, and an actual performance aspect of your daily life. For example, when I work with an athlete, I suggest:

- one affirmation that helps build the physical capability (strength, agility, speed, suppleness, good health, etc.),
- one that focuses on mental capacity (calm, clarity, focus, sustained concentration, visual effectiveness, lack of distraction, ability to block out external stimuli, etc.), and
- one that addresses actual performance (ability to perform a certain activity, like shooting the puck, making free throws, hitting a ball, making a smooth golf swing, making an effective presentation, negotiating a deal, selling your point of view, etc.).

The process can be applied to any situation with which you have to deal. It's simple and easy to apply. The important fact to remember is that it requires consistent and "hard work" to make sure that a massive impact is made on your subconscious brain. Your subconscious brain (the horse) is very strong. It requires a strong effort to move it to a new place in a logical, rational and conscious way. Sustained effort is required to effect the transformation to a new mental model.

APPENDIX 6

Visualizing for Effective Reprogramming

Another aspect in the process of reprogramming our subconscious brain (the horse) is the use of visualization. As your subconscious brain does not know the difference between what is imagined and what is real, it's a powerful method to help yourself unlearn and relearn in a non-destructive way.

The visualization technique stems from the work of Johannes Schultz, who developed the understanding about autogenic programming back in the early 1930's. Through his research, he demonstrated the ability of our subconscious brain to work on whatever image was suggested to it. Tests were done with athletes in various sports activities that showed the impact of preplaying a performance in one's mind through visualization.

More recently, extensive work has been done by, among others, acclaimed psychologist Lee Pulos, Ph.D., who developed a program entitled "*The Power of Visualization*" in which he details how we can improve our results through the power of imagination, by seeing what we will accomplish before actually doing it.

The following is the Amazon.com description you will find on the internet, of Dr. Pulos' cassette program entitled *The Power of Visualization* published by Nightingale-Conant in 1994:

> "SEEING IS ACHIEVING … one of the most powerful tools for achievement you have ever used. Visualization has helped millions of successful people achieve their goals. It can help you identify and obliterate the roadblock to progress, making your path to success so real that you can almost feel it, hear it, and smell it, as well as see it in the mind's eye. …this breakthrough program … will enable you to put this tool to work for you wherever there are personal challenges to be met. … Learn "The Power of Visualization" -- see your own success today."

AÏM FOR LIFE MASTERY™
APPENDICES

Suggested Technique
In my work with clients, I suggest that the following approach be rigorously applied to optimize the capability to preview performance:

1. Make a short video of your desired performance – visualize a play (in sports), a situation (in business) or an event (common everyday life) which you want to have happen instead of the weak and sometimes undesirable action which you have been used to take. The goal is to create an outcome that is in line with the application of peak performance. Include details that link to feelings of power, ability, skill, knowledge, whatever is required to create the desired result. Add as many details as you can, including something for all five senses. The more linkages you have to emotions and feelings, the stronger the impact of the visualization will be.

    This video of yourself in action should be a maximum of 10 seconds in length.

2. Run the video, forward and backward, slow at first then faster, to anchor the details. You now have a video of the performance you desire to produce. Every time you visualize the video, it should always be the same so that there is a uniform, consistent, and repeatable message sent to your subconscious brain.

3. Once the video is made, you can now run it when you do your mental programming (after relaxation and affirmations). It is recommended that the practice be done in two different ways:
    - first, watch the video on the main screen as if seated in a movie theatre, with no connection with the performance other than visual (**dissociated mode**);
    - second, transport yourself (in a swoosh) from your seat to inside your head in the screen, and run the video with full

feelings and movement, as if you were performing the actual action (**associated mode**).

4. Repeat the visualization exercise 2-3 times, each time you do your mental gym session, shaking yourself out of state after each run, so that your subconscious brain learns to step in and out of the performance state.

The visualization exercise should be run after you've induced yourself into the alpha state, preferably after doing your affirmations. The whole process should be a continuum from relaxation to affirmations to visualizations. The goal is to always do these exercises at a time and in a way that you get the best impact. That happens when you're relaxed, your mind is open to suggestion, and you're focused on improving your performance (optimally, before bedtime and when you wake up in the morning).

Doing the exercise at bedtime, you will allow your subconscious brain to continue working (dreaming) on the idea or thought. The recommended practice in the morning is to take advantage of the rested state in which your brain finds itself when you wake up. It is less cluttered with the daily routine and unexpected events encountered during the day.

Remember that, according to research, it takes 20-30 days for a new mental model (thinking pathways) to emerge in your subconscious brain. You will teach yourself to behave differently in current situations in which you have unwanted responses. Or you will learn an automatic and effective response for times when you want the capability to do your best on command.

APPENDIX 7

Secrets of Peak Performance Communications

The following are summarized concepts that can increase your communication effectiveness if you integrate them into your awareness. In your life, you've experienced, consciously or unconsciously, all these aspects of communication either to your benefit, or to your detriment.

As in every aspect of performance, raising your awareness to the fact that these concepts are at work all the time will enable you to achieve greater results, and consequently, greater satisfaction in everything you do.

The key is to be aware, and be flexible. We're all different, coming from different backgrounds. It's critical to include context when reviewing these concepts. Depending on the context, it may be necessary to extract a different meaning as a situation arises. In the end, it's always your responsibility to use this knowledge to improve communications.

A. **The Predominant Modalities in Communications for Humans**

   1. **Visual**   A visual person will tend to:
      - conceive ideas through the process of visualization
      - transmit those ideas with picture descriptive words
      - usually speak fast
      - have an erect head posture
      - display an animated facial expression
      - look up when thinking about answers

2. **Auditory** An auditory person will tend to:
    - conceive ideas through the listening or hearing process
    - transmit the ideas with sound words
    - usually speak at average speed
    - adopt a level head posture
    - usually have a calm facial expression
    - look sideways to formulate answers

3. **Kinesthetic** A kinesthetic person will tend to:
    - conceive thoughts through movement of the body
    - express thoughts largely through feelings words
    - usually speak very slowly
    - often have her head down
    - display very relaxed facial features
    - look down to think of the answer to a question

Note: No one is all one way or the other; we all display these traits at one point or another depending on the situations or context. The important point to remember is that persons have a main tendency.

B. **The Operating Programs (called Metaprograms in NLP)**

Direction: The tendency of a person to move away from or to move towards something.

Reason: A person will tend to state necessity or possibility as the reason for actions.

Frame of Reference: People will operate either using the feedback from others to guide their actions or feelings, or will simply rely on their personal convictions to guide themselves.

Convincer: A person will either be easy to convince or will never be convinced. Different degrees of proof are obviously required.

Relationship: The way to interpret things around us can range from total resemblance or similarity to other things, or total difference or dissimilarity with other things.

Attention: People will operate either from a basis of attention to themselves or attention to others in their activities.

Note: As always, we are cautioned that very few people are all one or the other. However, recognizing these programs in the people we work, play or live with can tremendously increase our understanding of their behaviour.

C. **Interacting One on One**

  1. The Priorities: To ensure accurate and effective communication, it is paramount that the right sequence be observed:
       a) the intention: what does the other person want?
       b) the criteria: what are the qualifiers of the intention?
       c) the content: what words are used?
       d) the process: what gestures are attached to the message?

  Note: Most often, people have a tendency to pay too much attention to the content of the communication (words) and forget the other parts.

  2. A Connecting Technique: Adopting an approach which leads to bringing the two parties to the same level of comfort through gestures. This is called "mirroring". It consists of duplicating the other person's gestures, in a delayed fashion, to send a subconscious message to the other person's brain.

Without noticing it, the receiver develops a sense that the imitator is connected to him or her.

3. Taking Responsibility: A successful communicator always takes 100% responsibility for receiving and making sure he/she understands. In the same fashion, the winning communicator will ensure that he/she has understood the other person's message correctly.

D. The **Mind-body Connection:** The knowledge and realization that both work in unison will serve as a tool to enhance our mental or physical state when we need peak performance to accomplish an activity. The mind-body connection is a concept that Herbert Benson, M.D., cardiologist and founder of the Mind/Body Medical Institute at Massachusetts General Hospital in Boston, and Associate Professor of Medicine at Harvard Medical School has made common place in his study of the relaxation response.

Effective Listening Gestures

As listening is a critical component of effective communication for peak performance, it is important to increase your awareness of techniques that can help make it a personal strength in your journey to excellence.

The following are six gestures that could dramatically improve your ability to listen effectively. This information is inspired from an audio program by Ron Meiss entitled *Effective Listening* Skills published by CareerTrack. This recipe aimed at improving listening skills and making you a better communicator, is easily remembered by the acronym LISTEN. When you are listening, it will make things more interesting, and possibly will help you gain more from the times that you are receiving information.

AÏM FOR LIFE MASTERY™
APPENDICES

A Recipe for Effective Listening

L - lean forward. This is an effective way to send a message to the
speaker and to yourself that you are interested. It predisposes
your physiological hearing to be attentive to the words and
gestures.

I - involved posture. When you are talking to someone, do you feel that
the other person is listening if she is turned away from you? If
the behaviour is maintained, I'm sure that there comes a point in
time where you will think that your communication effort is futile.
Therefore, when you're listening, make sure that your shoulders
are squarely facing the speaker.

S - smile. It is said that a smile is the reflection of the heart. It's the best
tool to give respect and acceptance to the speaker. It's also the
most powerful tool to encourage people to open up and have a
frank conversation.

T - territory, distance. In communication, the flow will be helped or
hindered by the speaker's level of comfort. If we get too close to
a stranger, he is likely to be constrained by the discomfort of
closeness, and the message will not be captured. The same
applies when we stay too far from the speaker. It sends a
message that we're not comfortable and therefore reduces the
effectiveness. Applied to our North American culture, distances
vary for the degree of familiarity with the speaker. For intimate
friends, the territory within three feet is common. For
acquaintances, three to five feet would normally be comfortable.
When it comes to business encounters, five to ten feet would
give a measure of latitude. Anything beyond is associated with
strangers.

E - eye contact. Since gestures are so important in the context of communication, seeing the speaker will go a long way to clarify the message. In a normal situation, eye contact should be maintained for at least 60 percent of the time. Besides allowing the listener to read the body language, eye contact also gives a sense of connectedness to the speaker. It sends a message that the listener is interested in the communication and wants to understand.

N - non-distracting gestures. Of course, if we are to be effective listeners, we will avoid creating distractions for the speaker. Playing with a pen, shuffling papers, scratching one's face, rolling the eyes are a few of the gestures that can surely take a speaker off course. The objective is to use non-distracting gestures if we are to reinforce our silent message of encouragement. One might be to nod the head once in a while to express agreement or understanding.

These gestures are meant to help us become more effective in our listening process. As with any other skill, it may not be easy at first. But the rewards are very significant. Learning to better understand others and helping others to communicate with us can make a big difference in the success of our efforts.

Try some of these techniques with friends. Tell them you're practicing effective listening. Get their impression of the approach as they perceive it when you use it. It may be hard work at first. Don't despair! The law of practice says that if you practice long enough, it will become easy. Think of your own experience. Surely, there's at least one skill you've mastered just by doing it, not necessarily because you liked it. Fake it till you make it! You will reap the rewards of mastering effective listening skills.

APPENDIX 8

The ABC of Emotional Mastery

It's been said that our ability to perform is based on intelligence and emotions. Research has shown that about 20 percent is due to IQ (intelligence quotient) and 80 percent to EQ (emotional quotient). These capabilities allow us to face challenges daily in an efficient and effective way or in the contrary, cause us to have unwanted results.

The ABC concept was originated by Albert Ellis, author of "*The Guide to Rational Living*" in 1957. His research led to the science of Rational Emotive Behaviour Therapy (REBT). Ellis' theory explains that all emotional outbursts follow the same path in producing a visible physical reaction to any stimulus. Stimulus here means any event, thing, word, action that touches our five senses and generates a reaction (cause and effect). Developing the ability to respond appropriately to the stimulus is called "response-ability" (Stephen Covey – *The 7 Habits of Highly Effective People*).

The path follows a well-established sequence:

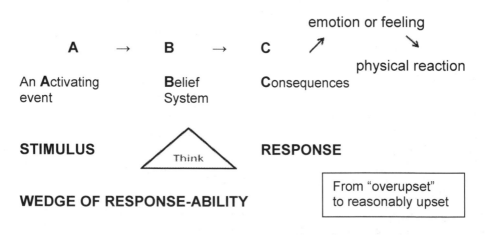

AÏM FOR LIFE MASTERY™
APPENDICES

Our senses are touched by an external stimulus which causes us to be happy, sad, angry, frustrated, determined, whatever emotion surges in us because of the impact. The consequence is a response to the stimulus. The important thing to remember is that we are human, and therefore will always react to a stimulus (our belief system or past experience puts an interpretation on every stimulus). However, the key, as Ellis points out, is to reduce the degree to which we respond.

Tom Miller, in his program *Self-Discipline and Emotional Control*, talks about moving from "overupset" to "reasonably upset", which leads to a more appropriate response. The way to create that appropriate response is to take the time to think (the wedge to create space between stimulus and response) and rationally determine the severity of the event and its impact.

The Thinking Wedge
In order to create response-ability, Miller suggests the use of two pertinent questions:
1.   Is this true, real, makes a difference, is important, etc. ?
     IF **YES** – go to 2   IF **NO** – forget it, move on, calm down

2.   Does it help me reach my goals ?
     IF **YES** – take a serious look at what action you will take.
     IF **NO** – move on, forget it.

Once you learn to take the time to ask these questions when faced with an emotionally charged situation, you will gain mastery of the reflex response. You will learn to inject Emotional Intelligence in your way of doing. You will move closer to peak performance.

Copyright 1996
Raymond Perras

APPENDIX 9

Decision Analysis Template

	Decision to take:				

Rank	Option 1	Go/ No Go	Option 2	Go/ No Go
Musts				

High Wants		Weight	Probability	Rating		Weight	Probability	Rating

Medium Wants								
Low Wants								
	TOTAL SCORE				**TOTAL SCORE**			

Notes:
1. A clear and well-defined description of the desired decision is the first priority.
2. Option 1, 2, 3, .., are the potential choices. Example, buying a car – choices are Honda Civic, Toyota Corolla or Hyundai Elantra.
3. MUST is a sine qua non criteria - the option is not acceptable if a MUST is a NO GO (e.g., price, space, etc).
4. Judgement is applied to the following considerations:

   Weight = severity, seriousness, impact of the aspect (apply 1 to 10 for low to high)
   Probability = likelihood that this will happen (apply 1 to 10 for low to high)

   Weight X Probability = Rating. The total determines which option will be selected.

APPENDIX 10

Life Successes Inventory

Life Successes Inventory		
List all Accomplishments	Personal feelings / What I learned	List the Impact / Benefits

<u>Suggestion</u>:

Take time to reflect on the successes you have created in your life. Think of family, parents, community, sports, school, career, relationships, friendships, special projects, financial deals, volunteer work, leadership roles, helping the less fortunate, speaking out, earning honours and any other accomplishment that makes you proud. List them. Then fill out the next two columns.

You will soon realize what you are really good at, and you will discover your ideal profession or desired domain of work.

Raymond Perras is a certified professional coach with over fifteen years experience coaching individuals and organizations in peak performance in both business and sports.

As a professional engineer, he managed many projects involving a variety of disciplines, skills, expertise and abilities. On the sports side, his involvement spans over 40 years as a player, coach and in the last 20 years, as performance coach in hockey, football and other sports from the minor levels to the pros.

Having witnessed the transformation of numerous clients from average to outstanding performers, he shares a process that anyone can apply to create awareness, internalize and integrate it, and master the knowledge to make it second nature.

In this book, the author provides the framework and the techniques and practices that can help you to install a program in your daily routine that will ensure uniform, consistent and repeatable results. You will create peak performance in your life by applying the elements of his definition: **the right stuff, in the right amount, at the right time**^{TM}.

Having learned from life that there is truth about the saying "winners make it happen, losers let it happen", Raymond has drawn a path to peak performance that enables you to build the capacity to influence your results. He is happy to share a simple recipe that requires hard work but leads to success in mastering your life.

Raymond lives in Ottawa, Ontario, Canada. His performance coaching business provides services to individuals, businesses and sports organizations in Canada and the USA. He continues to research ways and means to increase the value of peak performance through his work with varsity sports programs at the University of Ottawa, and with corporate clients seeking to increase results while reducing stress.

His next major goal is to write a book for coaching and guidance of the leaders who are charged with the task of creating a peak performance environment for their teams.